THE NATURAL WORLD
of
JACKSON HOLE
An Ecological Primer

by Tim W. Clark

To Denise

Originally published as *Ecology of Jackson Hole, Wyoming: A Primer* by Tim W. Clark in 1981.

ISBN 0-931895-51-0
(acid free paper)

Publisher and project coordinator:
Sharlene Milligan

Editor:
Denise Casey

Photographer:
Jackie Gilmore, *except as noted below.*

Illustrator and cartographer:
Lawrence Ormsby

Designer:
Carole Thickstun

Printing coordination:
Scott Kerby, Precision Litho, SLC

Historical photographs in Chapter 7 from the Collection of the Jackson Hole Historical Society and Museum.

Photos pages 40, 74: L.R. Ormsby

Photo page 30: W.E. Dilley, NPS

Photo page 19: Wyoming Game and Fish

Illustrations on pages 29, 45, and 51 by Wendy Morgan.

Contents

"God bless Wyoming and keep it wild."

Helen Mettler, who lost her life in Taggart Canyon, Teton Mountains,
August 30, 1926, in her sixteenth year.
The last entry in her diary before returning East the previous year.

It is a century now since Darwin gave us the first glimpse of the origin of species. We know now what was unknown to all the preceding caravan of generations: that men are only fellow voyagers with other creatures in the odyssey of evolution. This new knowledge should have given us, by this time, a sense of kinship with fellow creatures; a wish to live and let live; a sense of wonder over the magnitude and duration of the biotic enterprise. Above all we should, in the century since Darwin, have come to know that man, while now captain of the adventuring ship, is hardly the sole object of its quest, and that his prior assumptions to this effect arose from the simple necessity of whistling in the dark.

These things, I say, should have come to us.
I fear they have not come to many.

Aldo Leopold, A Sand County Almanac

The only real revolutionary stance is that "nature" is the greatest convention of all. Perhaps there are no natures, no essences—only categories and paradigms that human beings mentally and politically impose on the flux of experience in order to produce illusions of certainty, definiteness, distinction, hierarchy. Apparently, human beings do not like a Heraclitan world; they want fixed points of reference in order not to fall into vertigo, nausea. Perhaps the idea of nature or essence is man's ultimate grasp for eternity. The full impact of the theory of evolution (the mutability of species— including man) is thus still to come.

John Rodman, The Dolphin Papers

Preface

Jackson Hole's scenic mountains and abundant wildlife are unparalleled. However, some residents and visitors to the valley are better equipped than others to understand and appreciate what they see and feel of its marvels, its rich biota, and the interplay of dynamic physical forces. For some, an hour of viewing the blurred panorama from their speeding cars is long enough. For others, a lifetime is too short to understand fully the evolutionary drama unfolding all around them as recorded in the rocks, rivers, plants, and animals.

This book is an overview of the ecology of Jackson Hole and surrounding region. It is written for people who will spend more than an hour or two there. It introduces the reader to the natural world of Jackson Hole and to the principles of ecology as they operate in the valley. I hope this treatment will meet the needs of beginners as well as advanced students of natural history and ecology who are new to this area. I have drawn upon many ecological studies that have been conducted in Jackson Hole and nearby over the last few decades. References for these studies and more general references are listed at the end of the book. I hope this primer will help increase people's understanding and appreciation so that we can secure a healthy, spacious future for Jackson Hole.

Acknowledgments

Many people provided technical and moral support as I worked on this volume. Without their support, encouragement and direct assistance over the years, this book would not have been written. For this second edition, Denise Casey's editorial comments were essential. Several people reviewed the manuscript or supplied information: Bill Barmore, Franz Camenzind, Peyton Curlee, Jackie Gilmore, Rob Gipson, Pam Lichtman, Sue Lurie, Ann Mebane, Sharlene Milligan, Bob Schiller, Sandy Shuptrine, Bruce Smith, Bill Swift, Clare Payne Symmons and Darwin Wile. Many researchers in universities and state and federal agencies carried out much of the ecological work summarized in this volume over several decades. Jackie Gilmore supplied the photographs. Lawrence Ormsby and Carole Thickstun did the drawings and design, respectively. Thanks also to the Grand Teton Natural History Association board of directors and the National Park Service for approving the publishing of this edition.

Several people contributed to the first edition on which this updated and expanded version is based. They too made a significant contribution to this book: Jack de Golia, Bill Barmore, Pete Hayden, Tom Campbell, Marcia Casey, John Weaver, Joanna Booser, George Gruell, Chuck Spray, Garvice Roby, Nick Anderson, Wendy Morgan and Franz Camenzind. Thanks to all these people and others who helped in many ways.

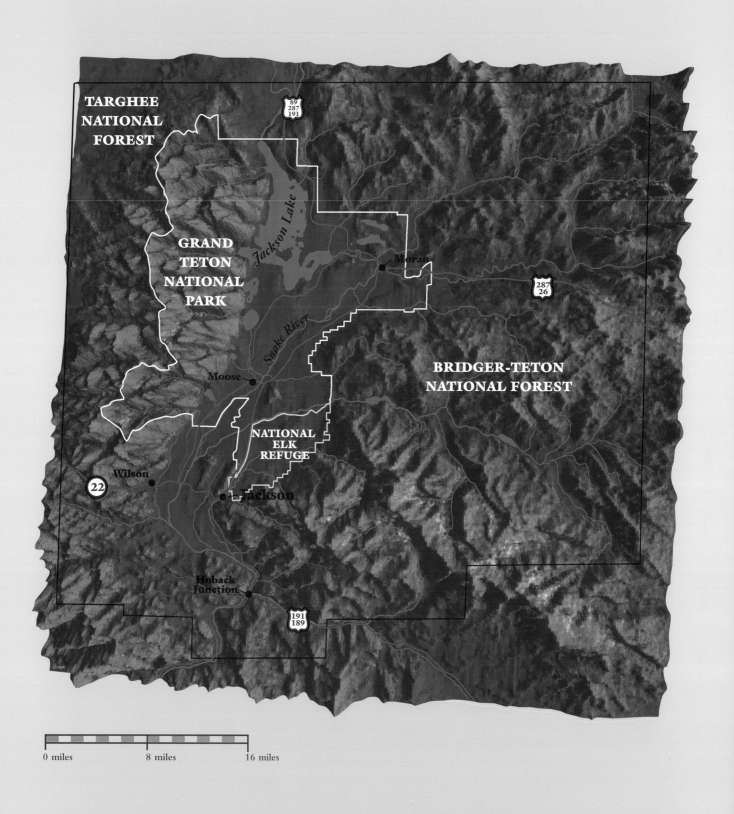

TARGHEE NATIONAL FOREST

GRAND TETON NATIONAL PARK

Jackson Lake

Moran

Snake River

BRIDGER-TETON NATIONAL FOREST

Moose

NATIONAL ELK REFUGE

Wilson

Jackson

Hoback Junction

0 miles   8 miles   16 miles

1.1 Jackson Hole. Black boundary indicates Teton County. White line indicates the boundary of Grand Teton National Park. The yellow boundary defines the National Elk Refuge.

Introduction

The magnificent Teton Range in northwestern Wyoming is one of the most recognizable mountain ranges in North America. Millions view its rugged, world-renowned peaks and valleys each year. These mountains, partly in Grand Teton National Park, are a spectacular backdrop for the valley to the east—Jackson Hole. This valley of over 400 square miles is rimmed by mountain ranges and vast wilderness areas. Yellowstone National Park lies on the high volcanic plateau immediately north. The mountainous Teton Wilderness area borders the northeast, and the Gros Ventre Mountains in Bridger-Teton National Forest lie to the east and south. The mighty Snake River, which originates in Teton Wilderness just south of Yellowstone National Park, flows through Jackson Hole. The valley lies near the center of Teton County, Wyoming (*figure 1.1*), which totals 411,535 acres or about 643 square miles. The western frontier heritage of this area makes Jackson Hole equally memorable.

Paleo-Indians used Jackson Hole long before the last glaciers melted from the valley over 7,000 years ago. Later it was a summer hunting ground for Blackfeet, Bannock, Crow, Snake, and Arapaho peoples. These Indians were part of the natural biological communities and did relatively little to alter them.

With the coming of European Americans, the ecology of Jackson Hole began to change, slowly at first but very rapidly in recent years. By 1825 fur trappers were removing many beavers, river otters, mink, American martens, and other animals. The valley was named for one of them, trapper Henry David Jackson. Settlement came late largely because of Jackson Hole's isolated location, deep snows, and long, cold winters (although these factors made it appealing to numerous outlaws who allegedly frequented the area). Cattle and sheep grazing altered many plant communities and affected many smaller wildlife species, such as ground squirrels, mice, and songbirds. Farming and logging further disturbed the natural environment. At the same time, hunters and ranchers demanded that government help to destroy large predators—grizzly and black bears, wolves, and mountain lions—by shooting, trapping, and poisoning, with a marked effect on many other forms of wildlife as well.

With the establishment of Grand Teton National Park in 1929, another force began to affect the Teton landscape—tourism. By 1950, when the park was greatly enlarged and rededicated "to the benefit of all posterity," tourist traffic was increasing steadily. With annual visitation in the millions in recent years and a rapidly growing resident population, human impacts continue to mushroom.

Yet the environment of Jackson Hole remains relatively pristine and continues to draw tourists and new residents alike, all of whom have a major cumulative impact on the environment. Many people, discouraged by the deterioration and loss of natural areas in their home states, demand that the quality of Jackson Hole and other vacation areas be preserved. Human impacts in Jackson Hole can be minimized by thoughtfulness, knowledge, vision, and planning, but these efforts must rest upon a sound understanding of the ecology of Jackson Hole and environs.

RECOMMENDED RESOURCES

Brown, T., Jr., 1983. *Tom Brown's field guide to nature observation and tracking.* Berkeley Books, New York. 282 pp.

Duffy, K., and D. Wile. 1995. *Teton trails: A guide to the trails of Grand Teton National Park.* Grand Teton Natural History Association, Moose, Wyoming. 163 pp.

Gilmore, J. 1991. *Welcome to Grand Teton National Park: An explosion of life and color.* Grand Teton Natural History Association, Moose, Wyoming. 12 pp.

Raynes, B. 1995. *Valley so sweet.* White Willow Publishing, Jackson, Wyoming. 177 pp.

Ecological Science

There is no better way to enjoy the beauty of Jackson Hole than to take to the trails. The pine and sagebrush smells, singing birds, and colorful wildflowers all make the experience refreshing. But an appreciation of Jackson Hole on this level alone is not enough to preserve it for "the benefit of all posterity." We all tend to view nature as segmented, made up individual parts—this elk, that lupine, this forest. Yet it is a far richer experience to view nature as a unified whole and to understand the interactions of all living things and their overall environment. An ecological view of the world is a systems view that includes humans and suggests what our role ought to be to conserve nature and ensure a healthy, sustainable future for ourselves. This viewpoint is essential to preserve the integrity of any landscape. An ecological view of Jackson Hole permits insights and understanding not provided by any other standpoint.

ECOLOGY AS A FIELD OF KNOWLEDGE

Ecology is the scientific study of the interrelationships of organisms with each other and with the environment. This includes interactions among individuals, populations, and communities, as well as the effects of myriad physical factors such as temperature, precipitation, soil, altitude, and latitude. The study of interactions of living *(biotic)* communities and their nonliving *(abiotic)* environment is the science of *ecosystem ecology*.

An *ecologist* is a scientist who studies the relationships among living things. Ecologists are sometimes confused with *environmentalists*, who act or urge the public and government to give high priority to maintaining a clean, undisturbed environment. Confusion arises because environmentalists often use the science of ecology to argue for environmental protection. At the same time, many ecologists—because of their studies—enter the policy arena to point out the far-reaching effects of human activities on the natural world and to urge protection of natural resources. Some ecologists are environmentalists and some environmentalists are ecologists, but they are not the same thing.

Ecology is a science that attempts to put all the parts of a landscape into proper perspective based on the best scientific information available. Ecology transcends traditional academic disciplines and draws from many of them—from atomic physics to mathematics and from anthropology to zoology. The goal of ecologists is to increase knowledge of the physical and biological forces that have shaped our world and our predicaments and thus give us a clearer view of our options. *Human ecology* studies the role of humans in ecosystems and landscapes.

Scientists recognize that matter occurs in increasingly complex levels of organization from subatomic particles to galaxies. Ecologists are concerned primarily with only five levels—organisms, populations, communities, ecosystems, and the ecosphere *(figure 2.1)*. An *organism* is one individual of a species (such as one wolf). A *population* is a group of organisms of the same species living in an area (for instance, two or more wolves). A *community* is two or more populations of interacting organisms (such as a pack of wolves preying on an elk herd that eats aspen). An *ecosystem* is a relatively independent, self-sustaining complex of interacting plant and animal communities and their environments. Jackson Hole is an ecosystem, as is the Greater Yellowstone Ecosystem, of which Jackson Hole is a part. Greater Yellowstone is a largely forested system of 19 million acres surrounded by flatter and drier lands. It has extraordinary geothermal features and a relatively intact fauna. The *ecosphere* is all the interacting ecosystems on the earth.

The ecosystem concept is relatively new. It was first used in 1935 to describe any discrete area, such as a forest, a pond, or a prairie, with a boundary, across which measurable amounts of energy and matter move in and out. The boundaries are arbitrarily selected by ecologists for convenience in studying ecosystems.

However, the Jackson Hole ecosystem does not exist in a vacuum. It clearly interacts with adjacent ecosystems, which in turn interact with more distant ones. The fact that these systems interconnect all over the planet lends stability to each system. Disruption of an ecosystem at one location can have unpredictable, complex, and possibly undesirable effects elsewhere. One objective of ecologists is to determine how everything in the ecosphere, including humankind, is interrelated.

ECOLOGY AS A SCIENCE

Ecology is a special branch of science that studies the structure and function of nature *empirically* (that is, through observation). Structure includes the distribution and abundance of organisms, while function includes their growth and interactions. As ecologists proceed in their studies from organisms to populations to biotic communities to ecosystems to the ecosphere, they progress from smaller to larger units of nature. Each succeeding level encompasses a larger variety of organisms and a larger expanse of the planet. The number, complexity, and diversity of interactions among organisms and their environment also increase with this progression. Ecology is a really a study of living systems over varying scales of complexity, space, and time.

The methods of ecological science can be descriptive or experimental. Much of the ecological study of Jackson Hole before the 1970s was descriptive, such as studies of Jackson Hole's elk by Olaus Murie that were published in 1951. Murie's excellent description of elk distribution, numbers, seasonal movements, and behavior is a classic even today. *Descriptive studies* document plant distributions, animal behaviors, or patterns of development of a biotic community, for instance, at a given site. The scientist does not interfere with the structure or functioning of the plants, animals, or communities. Even though much current study is still descriptive, more and more experimental studies have been undertaken since the mid-1970s. *Experimental studies* test hypotheses about the structure and function of the natural world, demonstrating particular ecological

phenomena such as population dynamics, competition, or predation. Mark Boyce's 1989 study of Jackson Hole elk population ecology, for instance, is more experimental and highly mathematical than previous studies. He compares elk demographics among years of varying winter severity, and he compares elk ecology and migration between herd segments in Grand Teton National Park and those on Bridger-Teton National Forest.

Some experiments require active manipulation of organisms or their environments. For example, a study on songbird competition may require that birds be added or removed from an area to achieve a known desired density. In this way, competition can be studied more precisely in several inter-species populations at varying densities and compared with a control (a parallel experiment in which the variable—in this case density—is kept at its natural level). In other instances, natural variations in plants and animals between locations or between years provide a "natural experiment" that scientists can study to test their hypotheses and gain insight. For example, the productivity levels of different meadows may affect the population sizes and densities of garter snakes that live there. Scientists can look at the ecology and behavior of two garter snake populations that are located only a short distance apart but occur at different densities to learn how plant primary productivity, prey species, predators, and other factors affect the populations' behavior. By the process of eliminating rejected hypotheses, we gain understanding and insight into the ecological world.

An *experiment* is simply a test of a hypothesis. A *hypothesis* is a postulated statement of cause and effect. It must be stated in words or mathematical terms that permit experimental testing. A hypothesis can be rejected, falsified, or disproved, but it cannot be confirmed, accepted, or proven with complete certainty by experimentation. For example, several alternative hypotheses may be offered to explain what factors regulate trout numbers in the Snake River. A well-planned and executed experiment can demonstrate

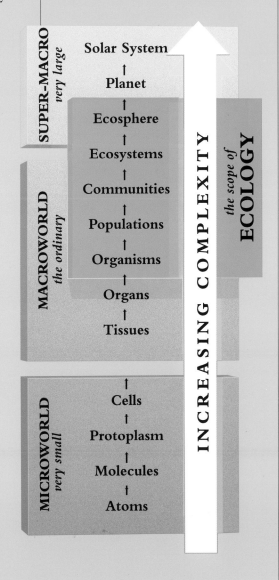

2.1 Levels of organization of matter

that one of the hypotheses does not explain the phenomenon, but it cannot prove which of the other alternatives (or some other as yet unknown hypothesis) is the operative explanation.

A hypothesis that survives many such tests, however, and is unlikely ever to be rejected is called a *theory*. The strength of a theory depends on the mass of supporting observations and experiments—or more accurately, tests that have failed to reject the theory. Ecological theories are interpretations of our accumulating observations about nature. Optimal foraging theory helps explain the foraging behavior of animals as they seek food, predation theory helps explain the relationship of coyotes and their prey on the National Elk Refuge, and competition theory provides insight into the distribution and abundance of different species of willows in Jackson Hole. Results of hypothesis-testing experiments may result in modifying a theory or adopting a new one altogether. This process of hypothesis generation and testing, theory development, and theory modification goes on endlessly. This is how scientific knowledge advances. Theories in all fields of human experience form the basis of our view of the world. Perhaps the most important ecological theory is the modern theory of biological evolution.

Models are important tools to aid ecologists' understanding of plant and animal systems. A *model* is a simplified representation of a natural phenomenon which may be written, verbal, graphic, mechanical, or mathematical. It is devised to provide insight into nature. Some of the most complex models are computer representations. For example, a computer model was developed to simulate American martens' vulnerability to local extinction from trapping and logging. The data used in this model came from field studies in Jackson Hole. Observation and experimentation can be used to verify, validate, and refine models to make sure they are reasonable and accurate representations of system behavior.

Learning to do good ecological science requires study and practice *(figure 2.2)*. The best way to learn about science is to study in school, read books, and work with experienced scientists. Most ecological scientists work in universities, research divisions of government agencies, or nongovernmental organizations. A number of excellent books give advice, describe methods, and offer perspectives on science and how to conduct it successfully. Developing an intimate knowledge of plants and animals, being a good naturalist and detailed observer, and experiencing nature in diverse settings are essential to becoming a successful ecologist.

RECOMMENDED RESOURCES

Begon, M., J. L. Harper, and C. R. Townsend. 1986. *Ecology: Individuals, populations, and communities.* Sinauer Associates, Sunderland, Mass. 876 pp.

Brewer, R. 1988. *The science of ecology.* Saunders College Publishing, New York. 907 pp.

Forman, R. T., and M. Godron. 1986. *Landscape ecology.* John Wiley and Sons, New York. 619 pp.

Marshall, K. G., D. H. Knight, and W. J. Barmore, Jr. 1979. *An indexed and annotated bibliography on the ecology of Grand Teton National Park.* University of Wyoming and National Park Service Research Center, Grand Teton National Park, Moose, Wyoming. 106 pp.

Smith, R. L. 1977. *Elements of ecology and field biology.* Harper and Row, New York. 497 pp.

University of Wyoming and National Park Service Research Center. 1994. *18th annual report.* Grand Teton National Park, Moose, Wyoming. 165 pp.

2.2 Students at Teton Science School survey aquatic life in a field ecology course

The Physical Environment

Storm clouds gather over the Teton Range

The physical environment of Jackson Hole and surrounding areas is complex and varied. Temperature, precipitation, ice, wind, geologic forces, soils, and water all affect the diverse species and the mosaic of biotic communities covering the landscape.

PHYSIOGRAPHY

The 40-mile long Teton Range dominates the Jackson Hole landscape *(figure 3.1)*. Elevation of peaks decreases north and south from the centrally located Grand Teton at 13,770 feet. Dozens of peaks exceed 10,000 feet. Along its eastern front the Teton Range rises abruptly, while on its western side the range slopes more gradually from the high peaks on the Wyoming border to Pierre's Hole (or Teton Valley) in Idaho. There are eleven major physiographic regions in the Teton landscape *(figure 3.2)*.

The floor of Jackson Hole is approximately 6,500 feet above sea level. It slopes gently from north to south and from east to west and has been ridged, grooved, and cut by rivers and glaciers. At its southern end are East and West Gros Ventre, Miller, and Blacktail buttes, four steep-sided hills of sedimentary rock. Formed by ancient faults, these buttes were already prominent features in the valley when they were carved by southward-moving glaciers.

The ruggedness of the Teton Range results from its relatively young

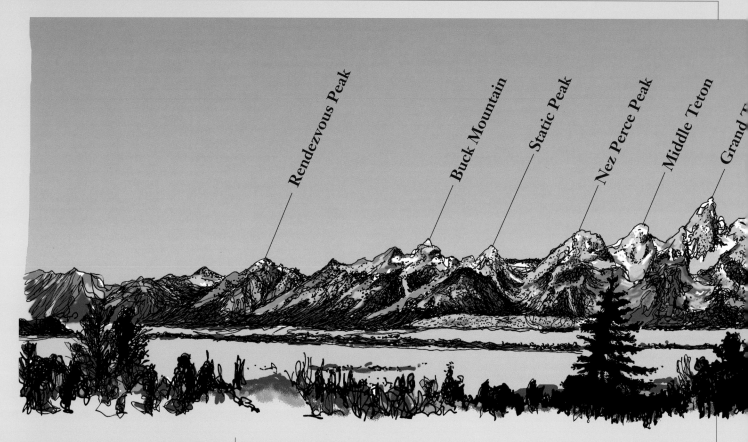

age (less than 10 million years), which has allowed little time for erosion of the very hard rock, which has no weak layers. In addition, the large amount of fault-block type of uplift that formed the range contributed to its craggy, irregular peaks. Finally, dynamic forces such as frost wedging, gravity, water erosion, and glacial action have worked on the mountains.

GEOLOGY AND GLACIATION

The Tetons are a fault-block mountain range *(figure 3-3)*. Part of the earth's crust fractured along a line and uplifted to form the Tetons, which are still rising about one foot every 500 years. Jackson Hole is part of the adjacent crustal block, which is still tilting downward along its western edge at the base of the Teton Range. The sinking valley puts tremendous pressure on the molten layers far below. The sinking

valley displaces the molten rock, which in turn pushes the Teton Range upward.

The layered gneisses and schists of Precambrian origin in the north and south parts of the range are estimated to be more than 2.5 billion years old, among the oldest rocks in North America. The granite and pegmatite of the central peaks are also about 2.5 billion years old. The prominent black band on the east face of Mount Moran is the outcropping edge of a dike formed about 1.3 billion years ago when molten rock was forced into a crack in older rock. Throughout the Precambrian era, from the creation of the earth to 600 million years ago, the Jackson Hole region was generally uplifted and eroded to an almost featureless plain.

During the next 500 million years, through the Paleozoic and into the Mesozoic eras, seas advanced and receded over this region. Thousands of

feet of sedimentary rock remain from the sand and mud laid down in these seas. But with the uplift of the Teton fault block millions of years later, these soft Paleozoic layers eroded and exposed the Precambrian rocks, although much sedimentary rock remains south of Open Canyon because of a fault running perpendicular to the Teton fault. Many aquatic fossils, including brachiopods, trilobites, and algae, occur in the Paleozoic sediments. Fish were common toward the end of the Paleozoic. Paleozoic sedimentary strata are visible from the Teton Village tram on Rendezvous Mountain at the south boundary of Grand Teton National Park and also in Alaska Basin.

The Jackson Hole region was changed from a marine to a terrestrial environment during the Mesozoic, an era of lush vegetation, dinosaurs, and coal swamps that thrived in the wake of receding seas. This sequence left today's landscape with both colorful and drab

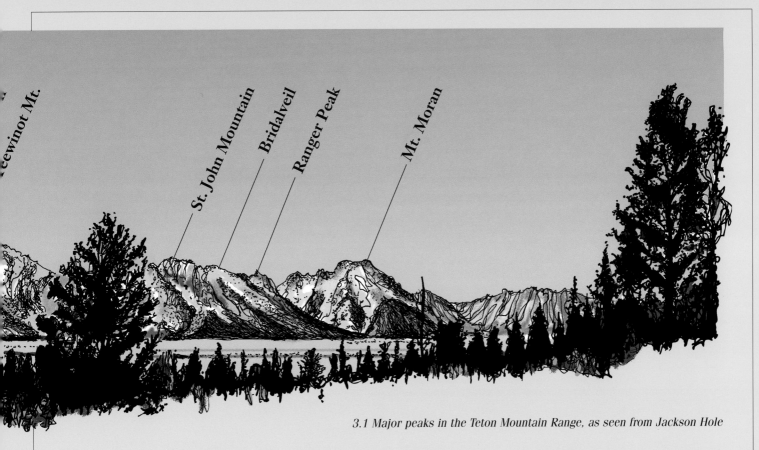

Teewinot Mt.

St. John Mountain

Bridalveil

Ranger Peak

Mt. Moran

3.1 Major peaks in the Teton Mountain Range, as seen from Jackson Hole

sedimentary rock strata, diverse fossils, and rich mineral beds. Mesozoic strata are visible along the east and north edges of the valley. Toward the end of this era 80 million years ago, broad, gentle crustal movements occurred in the flat Teton region. These were part of the Laramide Revolution, the mountain-building episode that gave rise to the ancestral Rocky Mountains.

We have a much clearer record of geological events during the most recent era, the Cenozoic, which began 65 million years ago. This was a period of general mountain building and basin subsidence. The Laramide Revolution climaxed 50-55 million years ago and ended 45-50 million years ago. Material that eroded from

nearby uplifts and volcanic features accumulated while deep sedimentary strata sank in adjacent basins. Then 20 million years of volcanic activity again leveled this region. Between 10 and 5 million years ago, the Teton fault block began to rise and

Jackson Hole was a large lake. Fossils and sediments from the Cenozoic indicate that the climate was cooling and drying and that many mammals developed in the new land environments. Despite more faulting, volcanic activity, and two more major lakes, the last two

Teton Range

Jackson Lake

Fault running along base of Tetons

Snake River

Jackson Hole

BLOCK A

TETON FAULT

BLOCK B

3.3 A cross-section of Jackson Hole showing the fault blocks

Labels on map:
Teton Basin (Pierre's Hole)
Yellowstone Plateau
Pinyon Peak Highlands
Absaroka Mountains
Teton Range
JACKSON HOLE
Mt. Leidy Highlands
Gros Ventre Range
Snake River Range
Green River Basin
Hoback Range

0 miles 8 miles 16 miles

3.2 Teton County and the physiographic regions that define the area million years left this region with the general landscape we see today.

The Ice Age gave Jackson Hole its finishing touches. The Buffalo Glaciation 200,000 years ago, the largest to cover Jackson Hole, removed all the soil. The present topography, drainage patterns, vegetation, and human uses still reflect this glacial influence. The Bull Lake Glaciation 80,000 to 35,000 years ago was less

extensive, while the least extensive of the three glaciations, the Pinedale, added many touches to today's peaks, lakes, and valleys. It ended 9,000 to 6,000 years ago and strongly influenced today's vegetation. Pinedale glaciers formed the large, U-shaped canyons in the Teton Range, such as Cascade, Death, Avalanche, and Garnet, and left the terminal moraines that contain Jenny, Phelps, Taggart, and Bradley lakes. The Potholes in Grand Teton National Park mark spots where large chunks of ice broke off from the retreating glaciers and were subsequently surrounded by glacial outwash (gravelly debris) carried by streams from the melting glaciers. The ice chunks then melted, leaving undrained depressions or kettles. The soil covering most of the valley floor consists of glacial outwash.

Small glaciers, freezing and thawing water, avalanches, runoff, landslides, earthquakes, and other forces continue to shape and change the Teton Range today. Evidence that the Jackson Hole area is geologically young is conspicuous throughout the region. Soils are

immature, that is, they lack well-developed layers. The melting of buried ice has been so recent that glacial kettles are still deepening. The mountains continue to rise, and streams change course. Landslides such as the Gros Ventre Slide are active, and earthquakes are frequent, especially in nearby Yellowstone National Park. A great deal of subterranean heat gives rise to steam vents and hot springs such as Kelly Warm Springs and Flagg Ranch Hot Springs in Jackson Hole and the world famous geothermal features throughout Yellowstone National Park.

CLIMATE

Jackson Hole has short, mild summers and long, cold winters *(figure 3.4)*. The climate varies considerably within the valley primarily because the higher elevation of the southern Teton Range near Moose and Jackson causes decreasing precipitation from north to south and from west to east.

Typically July is the warmest and driest month, May the wettest, and January the coldest. Frost may occur any month. Cold air flowing from surrounding mountains causes very cold temperatures. For many decades the coldest temperature on record was -52°

F in December 1924, but in December 1978 the temperature plummeted to -63° F and in December 1983 it dropped to -53° F. Moose averages about 2° F colder and Moran about 3° F colder than Jackson.

Monthly precipitation is nearly even throughout the year, except for July. Abundant snowfall, which averages approximately 120 inches annually, accounts for one half to two-thirds of the total precipitation. Snow remains from October through April. In the high mountains snow exceeds 12 feet in depth and lasts until July. It accumulates to a depth of two feet (usually considerably more) on the valley floor. From 1959 to 1980 annual snowfall at Moose averaged 191 inches, and between 1951 and 1980 snowfall at Jackson averaged 89 inches. During these periods Moose received 21 inches of annual precipitation and Jackson 15 inches.

Relative humidity is generally low and averages about 55 percent. In winter it is about 65 to 70 percent, and in summer it is about 35 to 40 percent. Humidity is highest in the morning and drops throughout the day to lows in summer of about 20 percent.

Solar radiation or sunshine in Jackson Hole can be intense. At noon in the summer *insolation* (brightness of the sunlight) may measure 8,500 foot-candles on the valley floor compared to only 300 foot-candles in nearby lodgepole pine forests. Few days are without sunshine in spring, summer, and fall.

Solar energy (light) affects evapotranspiration, the rate

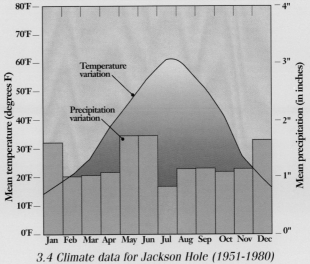

3.4 Climate data for Jackson Hole (1951-1980)

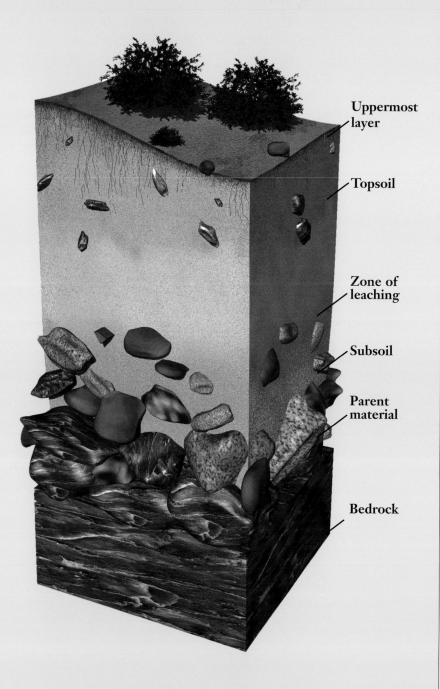

Uppermost layer

Topsoil

Zone of leaching

Subsoil

Parent material

Bedrock

3.5 A generalized soil profile

at which water is used and transported by plants. Potential evapotranspiration is about 19 inches from April through October. Frequently, a little shade is enough to conserve the limited available water. Snow persists much longer in shaded areas. The patterns of snow retention in late spring clearly correspond to patterns of shading as well as those of drifted snow. Vegetation can greatly alter light conditions. After isolated pine trees become established in sagebrush, they form shade patterns in midday that then influence the distribution of certain grasses and forbs (broad-leaved herbaceous plants).

The prevailing wind in Jackson Hole is from the west. Winds influence moisture distribution in the valley by controlling storm patterns and by redistributing snow after it has fallen. Precipitation usually accompanies strong winds in Jackson Hole. Wind is also important in soil formation. During past dry periods, wind carried fertile topsoils from Idaho across the Teton Range. This wind-blown soil (*loess*) was deposited unevenly across the recently glaciated floor of Jackson Hole with the thickest deposits along the east side of the valley. This process still occurs.

SOILS

Soil is a complex mixture of very small particles of inorganic material (derived from the disintegration of rock through weathering) and organic material (derived from living organisms), plus water, air, and living organisms. By volume soil is about 45 percent inorganic mineral material, 5 percent organic material, and 50 percent space between soil particles, which permits water, oxygen, and carbon dioxide to move through the soil. Plants and other organisms live and grow in soil.

The floor of Jackson Hole has poorly developed soils with a high proportion of rounded cobblestones from softball to basketball size. Ridges and foothill slopes have mostly fine-textured soils, but coarse-textured soils occur where erosion-resistant rock formations are exposed. Soils near watercourses range from cobblestones with sand and small gravel to sand, silt, and clay loams. Mountain soils are extremely variable, ranging from deep loams to very coarse textures developed from rock boulders and volcanic rocks.

The valley's soils differ in appearance, composition, and productivity. Differences are caused by the interaction of the original parent material, climate, relief, plants and animals, and time. Undisturbed soils are made up of a series of distinctive layers or *soil horizons* and the full set of horizons is the soil profile (*figure 3.5*). Most soils have three or four horizons, although some have up to six. The uppermost layer, the O horizon, contains decaying plants and live or dead animals. The topsoil or A horizon is made up of partially decomposed organic matter, some inorganic minerals, and the majority of plant roots. In the leaching zone or E horizon materials dissolved in water move downward through the soil. The subsoil or B horizon is the zone of deposition where organic compounds and clay accumulate along with iron and aluminum. This zone often has distinctive colors from the deposition. The parent material or C horizon is the source of all the above layers as it weathers and breaks down. The deepest layer is the bedrock or R horizon made up of impenetrable layers of rock. The deeper the horizon, the less influence climate and living organisms have on it.

Teton County soils in the area of Grand Teton National Park have been mapped by the Soil Conservation Service (U.S. Department of Agriculture). Eleven major soil types are recognized in the valley: four types, making up about 40 percent of the area surveyed, are found in the mountains and foothills; three types, totaling nearly 23 percent, are located on buttes and glacial moraines; one type, constituting 21 percent, is found on terraces and alluvial fans (including irrigated meadows); and three kinds, totaling 16 percent, are found on flood plains (for instance, flat lands). More detailed and refined soil descriptions have been made within the eleven major types, resulting in 71 soil classes in the valley (soil scientists recognize about 15,000 different soil types worldwide). Each type has been classified for its appropriate land uses—homesites, recreation, wildlife habitat, irrigated hay land and pasture, and roads.

Soils vary in texture and color. Texture is determined by particle size: clays are less than 0.002 mm in diameter, silt is between 0.002 and 0.02 mm, and sand is between 0.02 and 2 mm in diameter. Depending on the proportion of clay, silt, and sand particles, soils are divided into sandy soils, loams, and clays. Colors vary depending on the amount of organic material, iron oxides, and other factors. The Soil Conservation Service uses standardized color charts to classify soils.

RIVERS, CREEKS, AND LAKES

Most water that drains through Jackson Hole comes from heavy winter snows on Bridger-Teton National Forest (*figure 3.6*). The complex of water-retaining vegetation and human regulation of the Jackson Lake Dam both help maintain a relatively even runoff and prevent floods. Water is temporarily slowed by the vegetation, percolates through the porous soils, and rises again in clear, cold springs that maintain the relatively constant stream flows throughout the region.

The eroding rock formed from sediment laid down in ancient seas now yields valuable minerals to the waters of the valley. These enriched waters promote abundant plant growth, providing the foundation of food webs in the aquatic communities.

The lake basins in Jackson Hole were gouged out by glaciers that originated in the Teton Range and in regions to the north. Most of the more than 100 lakes and ponds in the region are in Bridger-Teton National Forest.

Jackson Lake, the largest in the valley, is more than five times larger than all other lakes in Grand Teton National Park combined. At high water, it has approximately 78 miles of shoreline and covers about 25,730 acres with an average depth of 123 feet and a maximum depth of about 445 feet. The two basins of Jackson Lake were excavated by the Pinedale ice sheet. The lake was enlarged in 1916 by damming the Snake River to ensure irrigation for Idaho agriculture. Managed by the U.S. Water and Power Resource Service (formerly Bureau of Reclamation), it fills during June and is drawn down about 10 feet by early September.

The water in large lakes such as Jackson Lake has several temperature layers that influence aquatic life. Plants and animals grow more rapidly in warmer water, for instance. Once in spring and again in fall, surface and deeper layers reach the same temperature, and all the water and nutrients in the lake mix—a process called *turnover*. Turnover brings nutrients from the bottom of the lake to the surface and carries oxygen to the depths. Ice covers Jackson Lake from mid-December to mid-May, and the lake warms rapidly after the ice breaks up. Temperature layering occurs by June and disappears in October. Oxygen dissolved in the lake is only slightly depleted during periods of stagnation between the spring and fall turnovers. Low concentrations of phosphorous and often nitrogen limit the growth of algae in Jackson Lake.

Lower Slide Lake, the second largest lake in Jackson Hole, was created in 1925 when a huge earth slide dammed the Gros Ventre River. In 1927 part of the dam broke, and the central area of Jackson Hole was flooded. Most of the dam remained intact to form the present lake of about 2,000 acres. Upper Slide Lake, a few miles east, was similarly formed by a different slide.

Jenny and Leigh Lakes in Grand Teton National Park, the third and fourth largest lakes in the valley, are typical glacial basin lakes. Because they receive their water from granite and metamorphic rocks, they are usually not as fertile and productive as lakes deriving their water from sedimentary rocks. Phelps, Taggart, and Bradley Lakes were also glacially formed, but their relatively shallow depths permit effective light penetration, making them more productive.

There are several smaller lakes in Jackson Hole, including Bear Paw, Trapper, and String Lake, which joins Leigh and Jenny Lakes and has a maximum depth of 10 feet. Two Ocean and Emma Matilda Lakes lie side by side in the northeastern section of the park. Holly, Amphitheater, Solitude, and Surprise Lakes are in the Teton Range between 8,415 and 9,603 feet elevation and are only a few acres in size. Because of their high elevation and short growing season, they are not very productive and are usually icebound from October until June or July.

All of Jackson Hole drains into the Snake River, the largest of the four rivers in the valley. The Snake River originates in Teton Wilderness, flows a short distance north into Yellowstone and then south through Jackson Hole, turns west into a canyon at the southern extreme of the valley, and eventually flows into the Columbia River and hence the Pacific Ocean. Several important tributaries from Yellowstone National Park and Bridger-Teton National Forest flow into it before it empties into Jackson Lake. Below Jackson Lake, three large rivers and numerous creeks flow into the Snake River. In its course of about 75 miles through Jackson Hole, the Snake is transformed from a small brook to one of the most important rivers in the western United States.

The Buffalo Fork River is the first major tributary of the Snake River in Jackson Hole. It drains much of the Teton Wilderness area northeast of the valley. After rushing down the mountains north of Turpin Meadows, it meanders through willow-covered bottom land until it joins the Snake a few miles east and south of Jackson Lake Dam.

The Gros Ventre River drains the mountains east of Jackson Hole, picking up many tributaries. It widens in two areas, Upper and Lower Slide Lakes, because of large landslides that partially dammed the Gros Ventre Canyon.

The Hoback River, draining areas southeast of Jackson Hole, flows through a high-walled canyon in the southern part of the valley. These rivers, creeks, and lakes—a product of physiography, geology, and climate—make Jackson Hole a well-watered region.

RECOMMENDED RESOURCES

Blackstone, D. L., Jr. 1971. *Traveler's guide to the geology of Wyoming.* Wyoming Geological Survey, Laramie. 90 pp.

Good, J. M., and K. L. Pierce. 1996. *Interpreting the landscape: Recent and ongoing geology of Grand Teton and Yellowstone National Parks.* Grand Teton Natural History Association, Moose, Wyoming. 58 pp.

Love, J. D., and J. C. Reed, Jr. 1968. *Creation of the Teton landscape.* Grand Teton Natural History Association, Moose, Wyoming. 120 pp.

Soil Conservation Service. 1982. *Soil survey of Teton County, Wyoming, Grand Teton National Park area.* U.S. Government Printing Office, Washington, D.C. 173 pp. + maps.

SNAKE R.

Berry Creek

Owl Creek

Moose Creek

Arizona Creek

Pilgrim Creek

Pacific Creek

JACKSON LAKE

TWO OCEAN LAKE

EMMA MATILDA LAKE

BUFFALO FORK RIVER

Moran Creek

LEIGH LAKE

STRING LAKE

Cascade Creek

JENNY LAKE

SNAKE RIVER

Spread Creek

Taggart Creek

Slate Creek

Ditch Cr.

LOWER SLIDE LAKE

PHELPS LAKE

GROS VENTRE RIVER

Flat Creek

UPPER SLIDE LAKE

N. Fork Fish C.

Fish Cr.

Crystal Cr.

GROS VENTRE R.

Fish Creek

SNAKE RIVER

Spring Creek

Nolan Creek

Sheep Creek

Granite Creek

Mosquito Creek

Cache Creek

Game

Porcupine

Horse Creek

Trail Creek

HOBACK RIVER

SNAKE R.

0 miles   8 miles   16 miles

3.6 Jackson Hole's major rivers, streams, and lakes

13

Plants and Animals

Jackson Hole is home to diverse plants and animals. Mountain meadows are full of wildflowers each summer, nearly 100 different kinds of butterflies live in the region, resident and migratory birds and bats are common, and carnivores like grizzly bears, mountain lions, and wolverines roam the backcountry. All these species have made adaptations to the cold, harsh winters and other environmental conditions.

SPECIES CONCEPT

Each kind of plant or animal forms a natural unit called a *species*. The species concept is among the fundamental concepts of biology. Species differ in their structure or makeup from one another. Differences may take the form

4.1a Uinta ground squirrel

4.1b Golden-mantled ground squirrel

of color or pattern differences, surface textures, relative sizes of body parts, shapes of reproductive organs, and other internal or external anatomical differences. Two kinds of organisms that are sharply differentiated are treated by scientists as distinct species. If their characteristics blend into one another or if they share some characteristics while others differ, then they are seen as representing variations or perhaps subspecies of a single species. The Uinta ground squirrel, for example, is a distinct species from the golden-mantled ground squirrel *(figure 4.1)*. The two species' overall body conformation is similar, but their appearance and life history patterns are strikingly different and they live in very different habitats.

Plant and animal species have common names, sometimes numerous and colorful names. The Uinta ground squirrel abundant in Jackson Hole, for instance, may be called chiseler, gopher, or picket pin. Because common names are not universally accepted or applied by any set of accepted rules, confusion arises as people in different geographic areas come up with their own local names for plants and animals. More than 200 years ago Swedish botanist Carl Linnaeus invented a system to standardize all plant and animal names. It is called *binomial nomenclature*. Every plant and animal described by science has two names. The Uinta ground squirrel (alias chiseler, gopher, or picket pin) is officially known as *Spermophilus*

armatus. Spermophilus is a Latin word meaning "seed lover," and *armatus* means "armed." The first part of a scientific binomial is the genus (plural genera) and the second part is the *specific* (or species) *epithet*. This name is accepted throughout the world and cannot be altered unless established international rules of nomenclature are followed.

Binomial nomenclature is also a method for classifying species into "higher order" groups of related species. Similar species are grouped in the same genus, similar genera in the same *family*, and similar families in the same *order*. The coyote *(Canis latrans)*, for example, is in the same genus as the closely related wolf *(Canis lupus)*. Both are in the Canidae (dog-like) family along with foxes. The Canids are in the Order Carnivora (meat-eating animals) as are the Felidae (cat-like), Ursidae (bears), Mustelidae (weasel-like), and other families. Similar orders are grouped together in classes; the Class Mammalia, or mammals, includes the Orders Carnivora, Artiodactyla (even-toed ungulates), Rodentia (rodents), Lagomorpha (rabbits), and others. In turn, similar classes are grouped into a *subphylum*, in this case Vertebrata. Similar subphyla are grouped into a *phylum*, here Chordata. And finally similar phyla are grouped into a *kingdom*, Animalia in this instance.

PLANTS

Plants are divided into several major groups, and one classification system separates them into lower and higher plants. Only the higher plants have bright, colorful flowers. Lower plants like algae or mosses reproduce without flowers.

Lower Plants—The lower plants comprise algae, slime molds, fungi (mushrooms), and bryophyta (liverworts and mosses). Very little is known about lower plants in Jackson Hole. We do not even know all the kinds that live here, although several hundred species probably exist in the region.

Higher Plants—Vascular plants have an internal system of conductive tissues to transport water and materials to all parts of the plant. This feature has allowed them to exploit a wide variety of terrestrial environments and to develop many specialized tissues and organs. Vascular plants are divided into three groups. The primitive and ancient ferns reproduce by spores. Together, the next two groups are known as seed plants because of the way they reproduce. The conifers and related plants (also known as gymnosperms) produce cones. Jackson Hole's familiar pines, spruces, and firs are all gymnosperms. Finally, the flowering plants (also called angiosperms) constitute the largest and most advanced group. It includes an enormous diversity of familiar plants—grasses, wildflowers, shrubs, and deciduous trees—but each one reproduces from a flower.

Nearly everyone has paused to admire Jackson Hole's wildflowers. But as botanist Richard Shaw has pointed out, the flowers are not there for us and their beauty is not for our pleasure *(figure 4.2)*. A key biological function lies beneath their colorful surfaces, beautiful forms, and enticing fragrances.

Flower colors and scents evolved to attract pollinators. Flowers are an adaptation for a plant's survival, and to understand them fully requires knowledge of the agents of pollination — insects, birds, mammals, wind, and water. In exchange for pollination, animal pollinators get food. In a competitive environment, each plant species has survived by developing unique features to distinguish it from other nearby plants. The coevolution of plants and pollinators has taken millions of years.

There are 1,056 plant species known in the Jackson Hole region grouped into 407 genera and 95 families. About half the total number of species are in seven families. The sunflower family (Asteraceae), which is represented by more than 160 species in the valley, includes such familiar species as asters and sunflowers (of course), sagebrush, fleabane, coneflowers, yarrow, and goldenrod. Dandelions, spotted knapweed, and Canada thistle are among the alien invaders of this family. The grass family (Poaceae) has nearly 120 species. The mustard family (Brassicaceae), with almost 60 species in Jackson Hole, includes alyssums, rock-cresses, drabas, and mustards. Fifty-five species of sedges (Cyperaceae), all native, are known in the valley. More than 50 species of the figwort family (Scrophulariaceae) grow here, including Indian paintbrush, monkey flower, elephanthead, lousewort, penstemon, and speedwell. The pea family (Fabaceae) is represented by 40 species in the valley, three-quarters of them native. These include milkvetches, lupines, and clovers. Almost 40 species in the rose family (Rosaceae) grow in Jackson Hole, including serviceberry, mountain mahogany, strawberry, cinquefoil, chokecherry, raspberry, antelope bitterbrush, and, of course, roses.

4.2 Fairyslipper or calypso orchid

Thirty species of vascular plants in this area are poisonous to humans.

One hundred seventeen alien species are known to have migrated into the region in the last 100 years or remain from earlier cultivation. The invasion of alien plants is of great concern to ecologists because aliens disrupt the ecology of biotic communities and may cause significant economic damage. Plant diversity can be maintained by monitoring species abundance, putting limits on construction, restricting horses in the backcountry, revegetating with native species, and removing alien species.

Even in an area as well studied as the Greater Yellowstone Ecosystem, there remain gaps in our knowledge of plants. Five new species of vascular plants from this area have been described since 1982; others have been discovered but wait to be described by science. There also seem to be some small plant communities in the ecosystem that, for unknown reasons, are separated from their usual habitats. For instance, a bog was discovered in 1984 that contains several boreal species characteristic of areas far to the north. In addition, basic ecological data needed for management and protection of many plants, especially rare species, is lacking.

Great gray owl *Strix nebulosa*
Hairy woodpecker *Picoides villosus*
Western wood-pewee *Contopus sordidulus*
Deer mouse *Peromyscus maniculatus*

Moose *Alces alces*
Uinta ground squirrel *Spermophilus armatus*
Belted kingfisher *Ceryle alcyon*
River otter *Lutra canadensis*

Oreas angle-wing butterfly *Polygonia oreas oreas*
Valley garter snake *Thamnophis sirtalis*
Muskrat *Ondatra zibethicus*
Boreal toad *Bufo boreas*

Elk *Cervus elaphus*
Canada geese *Branta canadensis*
Bald eagle *Haliaeetus leucocephalus*
Black bear *Ursus americanus*

Beaver *Castor canadensis*
Osprey *Pandion haliaetus*
Antelope *Antilocapra americana*
American white pelican *Pelecanus erythrorhynchos*

American wigeon *Anas americana*
Barrow's goldeneye *Bucephala islandica*
Northern pocket gopher *Thomomys talpoides*
Bison *Bison bison*

ANIMALS

Animals are divided into familiar groups taxonomically—invertebrates, fish, amphibians, reptiles, birds, and mammals. Some groups are comparatively well known, while very little is known about others.

Invertebrates—There are probably tens of thousands of species of invertebrates in the Jackson Hole region *(figure 4.3)*, although a complete census does not exist and an enormous amount of study would be needed just to catalogue what species are here. Arthropoda (invertebrates with segmented bodies and jointed legs) is by far the largest invertebrate phylum. The largest class in this phylum, Insecta, is dominated by four orders: Coleoptera (beetles), Diptera (flies), Hymenoptera (ants, wasps and bees), and Lepidoptera (butterflies, skippers, and moths). Together these orders contain 90-95 percent of the estimated 12,000 insect species in the region, with the remaining 5 percent distributed among 19-23 other orders. Butterflies are the best known of all the invertebrates. Other arthropod classes in the region are Crustacea (copepods, freshwater shrimp, and pill bugs), Myriapoda (millipedes and centipedes), and Arachnida (scorpions, pseudoscorpions, daddy longlegs, ticks, mites, and spiders).

Other phyla of invertebrates live in the Jackson Hole region. There are several dozen species each of Annelida (segmented worms) and Mollusca (snails, slugs, and bivalves) in the area. Other invertebrate phyla represented in Jackson Hole include Porifera (sponges), Coelenterata (hydras), Platyhelminthes (flatworms), Nemertinea (ribbonworms), Nematoda (roundworms), Nematomorpha (horsehair worms), Rotifera (rotifers), Gastrotricha, Bryozoa, and Tardigrada (waterbears). The Nematoda may include thousands of species, whereas other groups are made up of only a few species.

Most people are unaware of the vast biological diversity that lies literally under their feet and all around them. This diversity is essential to the functioning of the Jackson Hole ecosystem—and the world, for that matter. Invertebrates are overlooked, misunderstood, and understudied for many reasons. They are small, many species are secretive, and some live for only a few days. They are hard to identify. Their impacts on human activities are sometimes disagreeable. Nevertheless, they play vital ecological roles. They are critical to many food webs, they recycle organic compounds in decomposition, and they aerate the soil by burrowing through it. They are good indicators of environmental change. Conserving intact ecosystems is the best way to preserve invertebrates and other biodiversity.

Fish—Jackson Hole's fisheries are among the most prized in the world. The only native trout is the Snake River cutthroat *(figure 4.4)*. This fish differs physically from both the Yellowstone cutthroat trout to the north and trout to the south beyond the Palisades dam in eastern Idaho, although it is closely related to both forms. The Snake River cutthroat inhabits all significant waters in Jackson Hole, except for Emma Matilda Lake in Grand Teton National Park. Its current distribution is probably similar to its historic range, except for a few alpine lakes and streams where it has been introduced. For example, at least six Teton Range lakes now contain the Snake River cutthroat (Solitude, Surprise, Amphitheater, Marion, Holly, and Grizzly Bear Lakes). Overall populations have declined since pristine times because of the loss of spawning streams from irrigation diversion practices, introduction of exotic lake trout, other habitat loss, and fishing pressure.

Jackson Hole native fishes include cutthroat trout, mountain whitefish, Utah sucker, mountain sucker, bluehead sucker, June sucker, Utah chub, leather-

4.3 Spring azures

4.4 *Snake River cutthroat trout (courtesy Wyoming Game and Fish)*

side chub, longnose dace, speckled dace, redside shiner, mottled sculpin, and Paiute sculpin. Introduced species include lake trout, brook trout, brown trout, rainbow trout, Arctic grayling, lake chub, guppy, and green swordtail. The complex history of fish stocking goes back at least to the mid-1920s. An easily accessible, full account of fish stocking in the region would help us understand how aquatic and fish community ecology has been changed through this practice.

Mountain whitefish and Utah suckers are abundant in certain habitats. The rare leathersided chub is limited to a few small channels of the Buffalo Fork River. The June sucker is probably now extinct; no specimens have been collected since 1927. Brown trout are generally limited to Jackson Lake and more northern stretches of the Snake River. Lake trout are common in the larger lakes. Brook trout are also abundant in several lakes and streams draining them but rare in Jackson Lake. Rainbow trout are limited to portions of the Snake and Gros Ventre Rivers. Grayling were introduced to Toppings Lake east of the park and are found in Spread Creek and occasionally in the Snake River. Guppies and green swordtails were introduced into Kelly Warm Springs in the 1960s.

The major fisheries are Jackson Lake and the Snake River below the lake. Trout populations in both appear to be in equilibrium, more or less, with current harvests and regulations, although both the lake and river have changed over the years as fishing has increased. The most intensely used part of the fishery is immediately below the Jackson Lake dam; in 1973 anglers fished over 11,000 days in the tailwater. Fishing pressures has increased significantly since then, and virtually the entire trout population is caught each

year. Many fisherpersons catch and release. Fortunately, immigration replenishes the annual take.

Jackson Lake is also heavily fished. The average size of lake trout, common in the catch, has declined over the years. Besides problems with irrigation diversion, loss of spawning areas, and habitat loss, there are also problems with bait fish, the dam, and jurisdiction. Even though much of the Jackson Hole fishery exists in Grand Teton National Park, the state of Wyoming claims jurisdiction over all fisheries management in the park and has resisted attempts by the Park Service to share or influence those programs. Improved cooperation and problem solving are needed in managing Jackson Hole's fisheries, which attract thousands of people and large sums of money to the local and regional economy each year.

Amphibians and Reptiles—Until recently, amphibians and reptiles were little studied in the region, but recent research in Yellowstone and Grand Teton National Parks has made a significant contribution to our under-

4.5 *Wandering garter snake*

4.6 Sandhill crane

standing of them. Twelve species occur in the two parks *(figure 4.5)*. Given the size of the region, this low number is probably the result of the cold, dry climate and recent glaciation. All of these amphibian and reptile species are widely distributed over much of the western United States. They are all "generalists" that tolerate a wide range of living conditions. No turtles occur in the parks.

The amphibian species are the blotched tiger salamander, boreal toad, boreal chorus frog, spotted frog, northern leopard frog, and bullfrog. The reptiles are the northern sagebrush lizard, rubber boa, bull snake, wandering garter snake, and valley garter snake. In addition, northern Yellowstone National Park has the prairie rattlesnake; there are no rattlesnakes in Jackson Hole. Many of these species are associated with water, but some are totally independent of water.

Amphibians and reptiles are important even though most people overlook these species and fail to appreciate their aesthetics, their role in food webs, or their role as *indicator species* of an ecosystem's health. A brief visit to Kelly Warm Springs can be a good introduction to the frogs of Jackson Hole.

A world-wide decline in many amphibian populations has been documented in the 1990s. This decline may be caused by human alteration of global processes, such as warming, ozone depletion, increased ultraviolet radiation, or acid rain, to levels beyond the tolerance of these sensitive species. It may also be the result of some natural fluctuations such as drought. The causes of the amphibian decline are still being debated among scientists. Other human alterations of the environment that harm amphibians include draining or filling wetlands and using pesticides, which kill them directly and eliminate their food.

Birds—Jackson Hole's birds are visible and variable and can be easily located any day of the year *(figure 4.6)*. There is much diversity among the 300 or so species, and some species are represented by large numbers of individuals, such as juncos. They vary in body size and proportion, song, color, ability to fly, and behavior. They occupy virtually every habitat from riparian areas, to lakes, ponds, and nearby marshes, sagebrush flats and grasslands, forests and moraines, mountain slopes, subalpine zones, tundras, and towns and settlements.

Birds have fewer physiological adaptations than mammals and rely instead on behavioral means to cope with environmental extremes. Flight is the distinctive adaptation of birds that affects their occurrence, abundance, and observability in the valley in different seasons. Birds either migrate to milder, more productive areas in winter, or they tend to congregate around high-energy food sources in winter. Some species are year round residents, some nest and raise young here but fly south for the winter, some are seen only during spring and fall migrations, while others pass through Jackson Hole only rarely or accidentally.

A large number of species are associated with the valley's more productive lakes and the extensive river bottoms, wetlands, and mud flats. There are three loon species, six grebes, one pelican and one cormorant, eight bitterns and herons, one ibis, and 31 waterfowl species—including the largest of North America's waterfowl, the trumpeter swan. Three rails and coots, 28 plovers and related species, three phalaropes, one jaeger, and 11 gulls and terns may be found, along with the sandhill crane and occasionally the whooping crane.

Nineteen species of vultures, hawks, and falcons and 14 species of owls feed on small mammals, fish, or other birds, especially nestlings. Many other groups of birds can be found in Jackson Hole's varied habitats: six gallinaceous birds, five doves and cuckoos, two nighthawks, three swifts and six hummingbirds, one kingfisher, and 12 woodpeckers. A large number of small to medium perching birds are also found here, including 14 flycatchers, one lark, six swallows, eight jays, magpies, and crows, three chickadees, three nuthatches, one creeper, five wrens, one dipper, three kinglets and gnatchatchers, eight thrushes, four mockingbirds and thrashers, two pipits, two waxwings, two shrikes, one starling, three vireos, 19 warblers, two tanagers, and 53 species of grosbeaks, buntings, sparrows, blackbirds, orioles, and finches.

Mammals—Large mammals are highly visible in Jackson Hole, especially in winter when elk, moose, mule deer, bison, and bighorn sheep frequent the valley floor and lower, wind-swept slopes. In fact, large mammals are the drawing card that attracts many people to the valley. Jackson Hole is renowned for the vast herds of elk that winter here *(figure 4.7)*, and this valley and Yellowstone also have the only two free-ranging bison herds in the country. Grizzly bears, which have been absent for decades, are recolonizing the valley, and the wolves reintroduced to Yellowstone first made their way to Jackson Hole in 1998. But there are also many smaller forms.

4.7 A bull elk with velvet antlers grazes in a summer meadow

Like other groups of animals and plants, mammals have developed diverse life history strategies. Mammals, most of which cannot fly away to warmer climes as many birds do, have evolved a variety of ways of coping with the harsh conditions of winter in this region. Some of Jackson Hole's mammals hibernate, some migrate to winter ranges, some remain active in or under the snow, and some simply reduce the total time spent moving about.

About 60 mammal species are represented in Jackson Hole. They are grouped into six orders: insectivora, or shrews (four species); chiroptera, or bats (six species); lagomorpha, or rabbits and hares (three species); rodentia, the gnawing mammals (22 species); carnivora, the flesh-eaters (17 species), and artiodactyla, the even-toed hooved mammals (eight species). An experienced observer can find 20 or more species in a summer day. The abundant ground squirrels and chipmunks in the order Rodentia are easiest to find, although most people are more inter-

ested in the larger carnivores and ungulates. Mammals are found in all habitat types in Jackson Hole from underground in lowland meadows to the highest mountain tops.

Biologists use the term "small mammals" to encompass a host of mice, squirrels, voles, chipmunks, shrews, gophers, rabbits and hares, pikas, and related species. Often bats and members of the weasel family are also included. Although they vary greatly in size, most small mammals are inconspicuous, secretive, and nocturnal. With their high metabolic rates, these quick-moving, active species must eat a lot to stay warm. Their high energy needs dictate their life history patterns: many small mammals hibernate to reduce their energy needs, store food for use over winter, or forage throughout the winter in spite of harsh conditions. These forms are critical to the functioning of ecosystems. Their large biomass—a function of the large numbers of species and individuals—is a major component of the nutrient flow in ecosystems. They consume enor-

mous quantities of vegetation and invertebrates and, in turn, become prey for large numbers of predators. The numerous burrowing species improve the fertility, moisture content, and aeration of the soil. Small mammals also disperse seeds and the mycorrhizal fungi needed by many plants.

SOME CHARACTERISTICS OF ORGANISMS

All plants and animals have similar challenges as living forms in that they must take in nutrients, maintain proper temperatures, avoid being eaten, and reproduce. Each species has a pattern of life processes and behaviors that affects its fitness and efficiency in collecting and using environmental resources. The constant interaction between organism and environment is the basis for the continuous evolutionary pressure on organisms to adapt through their life history patterns. Ecology may be understood as the study both of environmental selection pressures that drive evolution and of the results of past selection as evidenced in adaptation. It is vital to maintain an evolutionary perspective in ecology when studying organisms and their environments.

Limits of Tolerance—The environment is like a stage on which an evolutionary play runs its course. Against the environmental background, biological processes such as reproduction, energetics, and parenting are acted out. The environment not only encompasses many abiotic factors, such as sun, water, and substrate, but also many other organisms. Abiotic factors determine whether an organism can exist in a certain environment: an organism that is not initially adapted to its physical and chemical environment cannot exist at that site, regardless of what other organisms occur there.

The plants and animals of Jackson Hole are more or less adapted to the abiotic conditions.

All organisms are profoundly influenced by temperature, light intensity, concentrations of oxygen and carbon dioxide, wind, exposure, chemical nature of the bedrock, speed of water-flow in streams, structure of the stream bed, soil type, availability of nitrogen and other chemicals, and many other abiotic factors. For each of these factors, an organism has only a limited range of conditions within which it may survive, flourish, and carry out necessary physiological processes. These are its *limits of tolerance*; beyond these limits lies the lethal range *(figure 4.8)*. Even within its tolerance limits, an organism is further restricted to a subset of conditions in which it operates at maximum efficiency. This explains why organisms tend to be found within only certain habitat types where abiotic and biotic factors permit it to exist. For example, certain kinds of bacteria live only in hot springs with certain mineral characteristics. This is also why Uinta ground squirrels hibernate—to take themselves out of harsh winter conditions in which they could not survive. And this principle explains why elk leave high mountain meadows and move to relatively snow-free, lowland meadows in winter.

Homeostasis—Maintaining Internal Balances—Organisms can overcome environmental limitations by assuming greater "control" over their internal physiological environment. For example, humans are warm-blooded mammals that maintain a 98.6° F body temperature regardless of external conditions. Animals seek to avoid extremes. Physiological constancy is their first priority; too great a change means death. *Homeostasis* is the tendency of physiological systems of higher animals to maintain internal stability. Having "control" of internal physiological processes protects an organism somewhat from external conditions. These homeostatic mechanisms are adaptations that permit organisms to expand their tolerance limits. By maintaining a stable internal state independent of external conditions, an organism is capable of tolerating a wider range of environmental variation. Of course, there are still tolerance limits beyond which homeostatic mechanism are ineffective. Even highly efficient physiological water conservation, for instance, cannot always save an animal in a severe drought.

Homeostasis has both physiological and behavioral controls. As warm-blooded creatures, birds and mammals maintain even body temperatures; control is achieved through physiological regulation of heat production and loss. The cold-blooded reptiles can only control their body temperatures behaviorally by moving into the sun to warm up or into the shade to cool off. Flying is a behavioral mechanism that permits birds to preserve their internal physiological status by moving from one environment to another daily and seasonally. Unlike most other animal groups, many Jackson Hole birds are migratory, moving to more hospitable climates in winter. Hibernation, migration, and other behaviors are ways that animals maintain homeostasis. A black-capped chickadee, for instance, will feed on high-energy suet in winter as a means of maintaining its body temperature.

Adaptation—An organism adapts to a whole suite of abiotic environmental conditions at the same time. For an organism to survive and reproduce, the adaptations that evolve from a given set of conditions must reinforce each other (or have a neutral effect). Thus an organism's life history is the product of trade-offs among reproduction (current and future), survivorship, growth, maintenance, competition, and predator avoidance. As a result, organisms show co-adaptive characteristics—often a

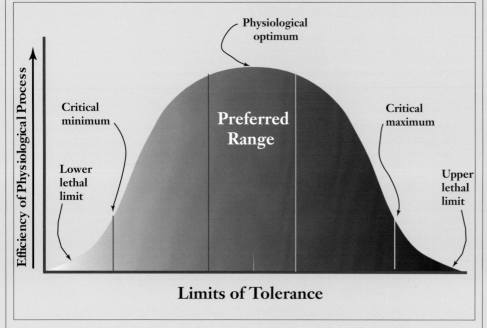

4.8 Limits of tolerance for the physiological processes of organisms

complex and highly adapted life history—that help them to adjust, expand, or displace their tolerance limits. A close look at any plant or animal in Jackson Hole offers insights into how the trade-offs are made and how adaptations serve the organism.

The relationship between an organism and its environment is not entirely one-sided. Plants and animals may alter the terms of their existence by affecting their environment. For example, a plant may modify physical conditions beneath its canopy and thus affect humidity, air flow, and other factors favorably. The beaver also significantly modifies its environment through dam- and lodge-building to enhance its existence in environments it could not otherwise inhabit. In short, the relationship of an organism to its environment is a two-way process. Initially, abiotic conditions set limits of distribution, abundance, and performance of species. In turn, once an organism or a population becomes established, it influences and changes its environment. This relationship is one of continuous interaction.

Life History—All organisms have a *life history*, that is, a characteristic pattern of life processes or behavior *(figure 4.9)*. An organism's life history determines how efficiently it goes about collecting and using the resources of its environment; an efficient life history conveys fitness. Resources such as time and energy are limited, so an organism must partition how it allocates its energies to vital life functions. Every organism's life history is tailored in a large degree to its environment, but some organisms are more efficient than others. In short, an organism's life history is a trade-off among many factors. Some life histories are very complex.

Organisms show two major kinds

of life histories called "r-selected species" and "K-selected species." r-selected species are generally short-lived. They have high reproductive rates and produce a lot of offspring with rapid development but low survival. Mortality among such species tends to be environmentally induced and is often independent of population density. r-selected species are generalists and good dispersers and colonizers. These species occupy temporary habitats (such as a temporary pond or a flowering forb community in spring). Insects are good examples.

K-selected species are usually long-lived. The birds and large mammals are good examples. They have low reproductive rates, producing few young and spending considerable effort and time raising them. Development of the young is slow. Mortality among K-selected species tends to be caused by competition, stress, or other factors that increase in importance with higher density. They are specialists and efficient users of their environments. Their populations are often at or near environmental carrying capacity and are thus resource limited. They are usually poor colonizers and dispersers.

calf

yearling

4.9 Three developmental stages in elk life history

adult elk

GUIDES TO THE PLANTS AND ANIMALS OF JACKSON HOLE

A number of excellent guidebooks have come out in recent years to aid in finding, identifying, observing, photographing, and understanding Jackson Hole's plants and animals. These are cited in the reference list that concludes this chapter. Most are useful not only to novices but also to experienced naturalists. These books provide common and scientific names, descriptions along with photos or drawings, identifying physical features, and status of the species in this area. The popular wildflower books are often arranged by color, although more technical floral handbooks are also available. The guidebooks to animals also describe habitats, activity patterns, feeding habits, and reproduction and development. Bird calls are usually described, as are mammal tracks and other signs. Maps and information on where to look for species in the valley are also given. Several books suggest driving or hiking tours for observing plants and animals, as well as other useful information, both ecological and tourist-related. The authors of these guides encourage readers to go beyond merely identifying species. They ask them to observe animal behavior, plant pollination, and ecological settings, for instance, as a means of increasing their understanding and appreciation.

Certain rules of etiquette as well as laws and regulations apply to naturalists. Picking wildflowers is prohibited in the national parks, as is the collection of any plant, animal, mineral, or archeological artifacts. Another cardinal rule is that many wild animals—not just bears or bison—pose dangers to humans, especially when approached too closely, when surprised, when mating season is underway, or when young are present. Observers should strive not to disturb or endanger any animals, remembering that environmental conditions may already be stressful for animals. Stay at least 300 feet from large mammals. Do not feed, harass, or cause any animals to flee from their normal activities. Natural environments should be protected, and existing trails should be used whenever possible. Finally, everyone from professional photographers to casual, roadside birdwatchers should respect the rights of other observers and landowners.

RECOMMENDED RESOURCES

Baxter, G. T., and J. R. Simon. 1970. *Wyoming fishes*. Wyoming Game and Fish Department, Cheyenne. 168 pp.

Clark, T. W., and M. R. Stromberg. 1987. *Mammals in Wyoming*. University of Kansas Press, Lawrence. 314 pp.

Clark, T. W., A. H. Harvey, R. D. Dorn, D. L. Genter, and C. R. Groves. 1989. *Rare, sensitive, and threatened species of the Greater Yellowstone Ecosystem*. Northern Rockies Conservation Cooperative, Montana Natural Heritage Program, The Nature Conservancy, and Mountain West Environmental Services. Jackson, Wyoming. 153 pp.

Dorn, R. D. 1988. *Vascular plants of Wyoming*. Mountain West Publishing, Cheyenne, Wyoming. 339 pp.

Forrest, L. R. 1988. *Field guide to tracking animals in snow*. Stackpole Books, Harrisburg, Pennsylvania. 213 pp.

Halfpenny, J. 1986. *A field guide to mammal tracking in western America*. Johnson Publishing Company, Boulder, Colorado. 164 pp.

Harvey, A. 1994. *The aliens among us: Introduced species in the Greater Yellowstone Ecosystem*. Northern Rockies Conservation Cooperative, Jackson, Wyoming. NRCC News 7:4-5,7.

Koch, E. D., and C. R. Peterson. 1995. *Amphibians and reptiles of Yellowstone and Grand Teton National Parks*. University of Utah Press, Salt Lake City. 188 pp.

Raynes, B. 1984. *Birds of Grand Teton National Park*. Grand Teton Natural History Association, Moose, Wyoming. 90 pp.

Raynes, B., and M. Raynes. 1984. *Birds of Jackson Hole: A checklist*. Grand Teton Natural History Association, Moose, Wyoming. 15 pp.

Raynes, B., and D. Wile. 1994. *Finding the birds of Jackson Hole: A bird finding guide*. Published by D. Wile, Jackson, Wyoming. 157 pp.

Shaw, R. J. 1976. *Field guide to the vascular plants of Grand Teton National Park and Teton County, Wyoming*. Utah State University Press, Logan. 301 pp.

Shaw, R. J. 1992a. *Wildflowers of Grand Teton and Yellowstone National Parks including the Greater Yellowstone Ecosystem*. Wheelwright Press, Salt Lake City, Utah. 64 pp.

Shaw, R. J. 1992b. *Vascular plants of Grand Teton National Park and Teton County: An annotated checklist*. Grand Teton Natural History Association, Moose, Moose, Wyoming. 92 pp.

Stelfox, J. B., and L. Lawrence. 1991. *A field guide to the hoofed mammals of Jackson Hole*. Teton Science School, Kelly, Wyoming. 50 pp.

Streubel, D. P. 1989. *Small mammals of the Yellowstone Ecosystem*. Roberts Rinehart, Inc., Boulder, Colorado. 152 pp.

Vogel, B. 1989. *Invertebrates*. Pp. 22-32 in T. W. Clark, A. H. Harvey, R. D. Dorn, D. L. Genter, and C. R. Groves, eds., *Rare, sensitive, and threatened species of the Greater Yellowstone Ecosystem*. Northern Rockies Conservation Cooperative, Montana Natural Heritage Program, The Nature Conservancy, and Mountain West Environmental Services. Jackson, Wyoming.

Wile, D. 1996. *Identifying and finding the mammals of Jackson Hole (including Grand Teton National Park): A field guide*. Published by D. Wile, Jackson, Wyoming. 139 pp.

Population Ecology

Plants and animals rarely exist as isolated individuals. Usually several members of a species occur together as a population. The single most notable population in Jackson Hole is probably the wintertime herds of elk on the National Elk Refuge. A *population* is a group of individuals of the same species that occupies a given space at a particular time. Certain characteristics distinguish populations from other levels of biological organization. Like individuals, populations have a structure, a function, and development and growth patterns. Unlike individuals that are born and die, however, populations persist, changing in size from fluctuating birth and death rates. In addition, populations are characterized by the number of individuals, density (numbers per unit area), age and sex composition, natality and mortality, and emigration and immigration. The biotic communities of Jackson Hole are made up of many interacting plant and animal populations.

POPULATION ECOLOGY IN JACKSON HOLE

Ecologists study populations to understand their structure, dynamics, and adaptations to their environments. Our interests often focus on this level, especially for wildlife management purposes. A brief look at elk, mule deer, moose, American marten, and Canada geese populations provide insight into this level of organization.

Elk—The Jackson Hole elk (or wapiti) population is one of the largest herds of native elk in North America *(figure 5.1)*. Elk range all over Jackson Hole during summer but concentrate in key areas during winter. On summer evenings elk can be seen from the top of Signal Mountain or near Timbered Island in Grand Teton National Park as they move from dense forest into meadows and sagebrush. In winter they can be seen up close on the National Elk Refuge bordering the town of Jackson. A refuge contractor takes people on sleigh rides through the herds for a breathtaking view of these magnificent animals.

Early narratives and journals indicate that elk were common in Jackson Hole during the early 1880s. There were 25,000 to 40,000 from 1900 to 1910 in the valley south to the Hoback Rim. Counts for several feeding grounds from 1912 to the present ranged from 9,346 in 1912 to 22,035 in 1935. More recently, efforts have been made to maintain the winter population on the National Elk Refuge (only one of the areas previously censused) at about 7,500 animals. But many years elk exceed this number.

The density of the elk population varies widely seasonally and annually. In summer, a population of 15,000 spread over 1,000 square miles has an average density of 15 elk per square mile. In

5.1 *An elk herd in Jackson Hole*

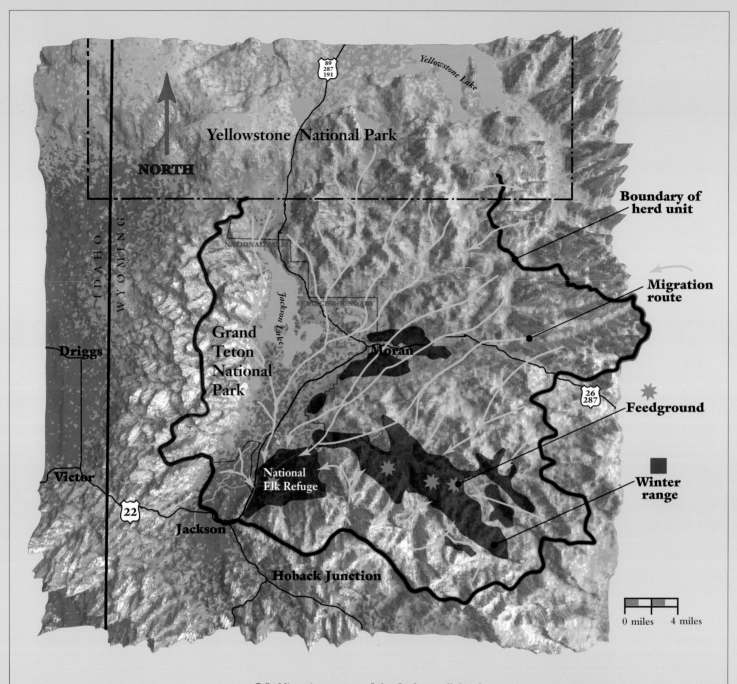

Map labels:
- YELLOWSTONE LAKE
- 89 287 191
- Yellowstone National Park
- NORTH
- IDAHO
- WYOMING
- Boundary of herd unit
- Migration route
- NATIONAL PARK
- Jackson Lake
- SERVICE BOUNDARY
- Driggs
- Grand Teton National Park
- Moran
- 26 287
- Feedground
- Victor
- National Elk Refuge
- Winter range
- 22
- Jackson
- Hoback Junction
- 0 miles   4 miles

5.2 Migration routes of the Jackson elk herd

winter the population concentrates on several relatively small areas. The largest is the 24,700-acre National Elk Refuge, where the population may approach 10,000 and congregate into relatively compact groups with densities occasionally exceeding 4,000 elk per square mile.

Elk originally summered all over Jackson Hole and surrounding mountains. They were common in central and southern Jackson Hole, and large numbers concentrated in southern Yellowstone National Park and on Big Game Ridge in Teton Wilderness. But increased hunting reduced their numbers in the more accessible central and southern parts of Jackson Hole. Today the elk that winter on the refuge summer in four distinct ranges: 48 percent summer in Grand Teton National Park, 28 percent in Yellowstone National Park, 12 percent in Teton Wilderness, and 12 percent in

the Gros Ventre drainage. Some elk travel as much as 60 miles between summer range in southern Yellowstone National Park and winter range on the refuge.

As late fall snows accumulate and reduce the availability of food, elk migrate to low-elevation wintering areas in the valley and to wind-blown, south-facing slopes *(figure 5.2)*. Migrations occur most often in November. Observation and counts of

26

elk tracks in the snow from 1949 to the present show that the relative numbers of animals using the migration routes have changed greatly. This coincided with a period of relatively high hunting kills. Segments of the population that migrated through areas closed to hunting (such as Grand Teton National Park) increased, while segments that migrated in heavily hunted areas decreased. Today managers regulate the different herd segments based in part on their migratory behavior.

Increasing human activity, agriculture, hunting, and the establishment of feeding grounds slowly altered elk winter distributions after 1910. The proportion of the population wintering on feeding grounds increased to about 50 percent by 1940 and to 86 percent by 1956. Today about 80 percent use feeding grounds, although small groups still use historic winter range away from feeding grounds.

The portion of the elk population that wintered on the National Elk Refuge from 1955 to 1967 averaged 62 percent females (including yearling females), 19 percent calves, six percent yearling males, and 13 percent adult males. From 1969 through 1989 it averaged 61 percent females, 18 percent calves, seven percent yearling males, and 14 percent adult males. Herd composition changed little from the earlier sample.

Mating occurs in early fall when mature bulls join groups of cows and calves. Bulls gather harems of up to 50 cows and maintain them against the advances of other bulls. The bulls emit a loud whistle called a "bugle" that advertises their presence to other bulls. Most female elk become sexually mature at 2.5 years of age, but about 17 percent are sexually mature at 1.5 years. About 78 percent of females older than calves and 87 percent of those older

than yearlings are pregnant annually. Conception occurs throughout September, and after 262 to 294 days white-spotted calves are born in May and early June.

Postnatal mortality of calves is 15-30 percent. The remaining 70-85 percent constitute the realized annual calf production. Predation, accidents, and diseases—strongly influenced by adverse winter and spring weather—kill calves shortly after birth. A small percentage of the population is lost from injuries by hunters, accidental death (by cars, for instance), and illegal kills in Grand Teton National Park. Hunters harvest about 20 percent of the herd. Only about two percent die on winter feeding grounds most winters, although 5 percent may die during severe winters.

Of prime interest to wildlife biologists are the mechanisms that regulate the size of the Jackson Hole elk herd. Different factors may have regulated the population in pristine times compared to those that operate today. Before white settlement the interaction of periodic severe weather, temporary food shortages, predators, parasites, and disease probably regulated the population. High winter mortality apparently occurred at four-to-six year intervals in the early days. Significant mortality is known to have occurred in 1882, 1887, 1891, 1897, and 1911. Predation, even by wolves, apparently was only one of the factors that controlled elk numbers. Predators, in fact, probably reduced competition for forage among elk during the most severe winters. The relationships between the elk and associated predators, scavengers, and parasites were probably helpful to all the populations involved.

Disease also affects the elk population, notably brucellosis (Brucella abortus). Since 1970 regular screening

for disease has taken place. Overall, about 28 percent of the elk on the refuge tested positive for antibodies to Brucella, including 39 percent of adult females. Large numbers of elk at 17 other feeding grounds also have brucellosis. Tuberculosis is another chronic, devastating disease that is not currently in Jackson Hole's elk but could infect them in the future. These and other diseases can have significant impacts on elk populations.

Today periodic severe weather, temporary food shortages, a more limited predator-scavenger fauna, parasites, and disease still act on the population, but human influences are the main regulating factors. These include artificial feeding, hunting, and usurpation of historic winter range for ranches, towns, and other developments. Sustained hunting harvests that more or less approximate annual herd increases and yearly artificial feeding seem to hold the winter population on the National Elk Refuge within the 6,000 to 10,000 range that has prevailed through the severe, average, and mild winters since 1961.

Mule Deer—Another visible winter population is the mule deer on the edge of Jackson and the slopes of the Gros Ventre Buttes (figure 5.3). Intensively studied from 1979 to 1991, this population's ecology shows a different dynamic from that of elk. The study methods included direct observations from fixed sites, aerial flights, live trapping, marking and release, radio telemetry, interviews with residents and hunters, and data from Wyoming Game and Fish Department. Deer were counted several times each week beginning in November each year coinciding with their arrival on the both West and East Gros Ventre Buttes and continuing until deer left in spring. Migration patterns, herd numbers, distribution,

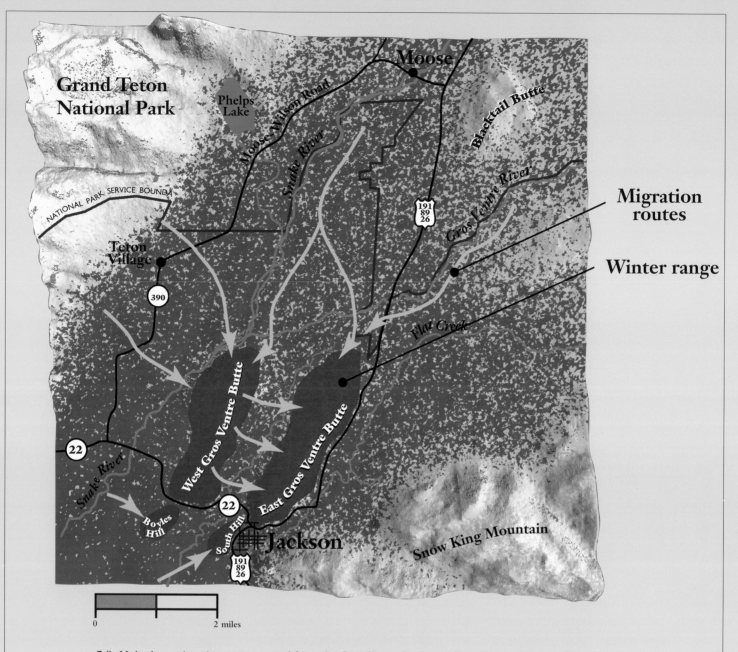

5.3 Mule deer migration routes to and from the Gros Ventre Buttes winter range in Teton County, Wyoming

age and sex structure, natality and mortality, habitat use, behavior, and relations to humans were studied, similar to the way they are for elk, and their ecology is fairly well known.

The onset of deep snows influences deer numbers and distribution. The maximum number of deer counted was 365 in 1977-78, and overwintering numbers from 1985 to 1991 ranged between 257 to 360. Peak numbers were counted in late January and early February most years. As the snow accu-

mulates, nearly all deer move to the south and east slopes of the East Butte and remain there. In January 1990, the herd consisted of 16 percent bucks, 41 percent does, 38 percent fawns, and five percent unknown. There were 68 fawns per 100 does and 49 fawns per 100 adults. The herd composition is similar to mule deer herds studied elsewhere.

Mule deer principally winter in three areas on the buttes—the east sides of West and East Gros Ventre Buttes and the south end of the East Butte.

Deer densities in the south end vary from one deer per 3.8 acres to one deer per 10.3 acres. This reflects the availability of food and cover.

Over the years of study, people sometimes fed the deer, even though this can be harmful to the population. In 1989-90 four artificial feeding grounds were operated by private citizens; about 32 percent of all deer were concentrated at these sites. Many areas of key winter range are abandoned by the deer in favor of provisioned food.

28

This results in local habitat depletion, increased disease transmission, and—if fed near roads—increased road deaths. Roadkills, in fact, appear to be the main source of mortality in Jackson Hole's deer population. However, deer also die from natural causes as well as hunting and unknown factors.

In winter 1982-83 deer home ranges averaged 198 acres with a range of 103 to 296, but in the following winter, they averaged 250 acres with a range of 62 to 328 acres. This difference probably reflects varying snow depth and availability of food and cover.

Deer used the slopes in diverse ways from year to year. Some years they use the lower slopes more, while in other years the upper and mid-slopes are more heavily used. This, too, is probably related to snow depth and availability of forage. Few deer forage or rest alone. In 1989-90 the number of deer groups—two or more individuals separated by no more than 55 yards—observed per survey averaged 24 (range 7-41). That pattern is typical for most winters.

Migration onto the buttes generally starts in November, but large numbers of deer are seldom observed until mid-January. Deer move to and from the buttes along well established migration routes. No large migration occurs as it does in elk to the refuge; deer travel to the buttes in small groups. They begin leaving in mid-March. In 1990 deer numbers dropped rapidly from 296 on March 6 to 154 on April 5 to 114 on April 26. The deer that winter on East and West Gros Ventre Buttes summer in an area of unknown size in Grand Teton National Park, Bridger-Teton National Forest, and private lands throughout the valley.

The population ecology of mule deer in Jackson Hole is similar to that in many other regions. Knowledge of population ecology can be used to understand the species and to devise conservation actions. For example, the results of this long-term mule deer study have informed efforts to reduce roadkills, encourage people not to feed deer in winter, and keep dogs off winter range.

Moose—The moose is the largest member of the deer family, which also includes elk and mule deer. Moose are prominent members of Jackson Hole's fauna and are readily observed throughout the valley in winter. They tend to use willow patches along streams in winter and spruce-fir forests high in the mountains in summer. Moose foods include subalpine fir, willows, aspen, and aquatic plants. Their noses are specially adapted to feeding on aquatic vegetation, and their long legs are excellent for traveling through deep snow.

Unlike elk and mule deer, moose tend to be quasi-solitary animals, but the movements of individuals typically overlap. Yearling males and adult females with calves show the least tendency to form groups with other moose. Agonistic (conflict) behavior is the major behavioral mechanism that regulates this spatial distribution. Conflicts are usually worked out through postures and gestures that indicate dominance and submission (*figure 5.4*). Most animal species have evolved behaviors for spacing individuals across landscapes as well as various other purposes.

Winter finds many more moose in Jackson Hole than summer. They move from higher altitudes to the valley floor as snows accumulate. More than 40 moose per square mile may occur where willows are abundant, such as near the Triangle X Ranch in Grand Teton National Park. In summer a resident adult ranges over about 1.5 square miles or less.

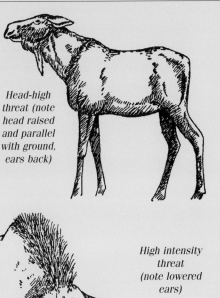

Head-high threat (note head raised and parallel with ground, ears back)

High intensity threat (note lowered ears)

Low intensity threat (note ears back, hair raised on neck)

Head-low threat. Medium to high intensity (note lowered head, hair raised on neck, rump and withers)

5.4 Some postures of moose indicating threat (Drawing by Wendy Morgan, after V. Geist, 1963. On the behaviour of North American moose in Birtish Columbia, Behaviour 20:377-416.)

The sex and age structure of the wintering moose population seems to be relatively constant at 42 percent females, 24 percent calves, and 34 percent males. Moose mate in mid-fall. Usually one young is born after 240 days gestation, but about five percent of the births are twins. Eighty-nine percent of all adult females and about 17 percent of the yearling females ovulate. Although 89 percent of the adult females are pregnant, the number of calves produced per 100 females varies from 49 to 66 in early winter because of post-natal calf mortality. From 1962 to 1966, for example, over-winter mortality of calves varied from 0 to 50 percent. Parasites, diseases, and non-human predation had little direct effect on total mortality rates.

Many factors interact to regulate moose numbers *(figure 5.5)*, including the quality and quantity of available forage, snow conditions, grazing by other ungulates, human developments, ovulation and pregnancy rates, diseases and parasites, and social organization.

American Marten—American martens are weasel-like furbearers of coniferous forests *(figure 5.6)*. Their rich, lustrous brown fur has long been prized and is still commercially valuable. Martens range from one to three pounds. They eat small mammals, including red squirrels. The population ecology of Jackson Hole martens is similar to the ecology of martens elsewhere.

Throughout the mid-1970s this species was studied at four sites in Teton County. Martens in Grand Teton National Park were totally protected, but those at three sites on Bridger-

5.6 American marten

Teton National Forest were trapped for their fur. Each adult male used about 500 acres and overlapped the ranges of two or three females, which used about 200 acres each. More males than females were live-captured and released, probably because males have larger ranges and likely encounter live traps more often. Of 37 martens (27 males and 10 females) whose ages were determined by teeth growth rings, 12 males were less than one year old and two were 9-10 years old. Six females were less than 1 year old and one was 12-13 years old.

In any one area there is a small semi-permanent population and a few other animals moving through the area, staying only a few days to a few weeks. Most movement occurs in November each year as animals seek good over-wintering ranges.

This kind of information reveals how a solitary forest carnivore's population is structured and how it behaves over time. Martens regulate themselves spatially through the establishment of territories, which, in turn, greatly affects how many martens will occupy an area, densities, birth and death rates, and migration patterns. Combined with other information, these data are used to determine the effects of habitat changes (such as logging) and random events (such as diseases) on small marten populations.

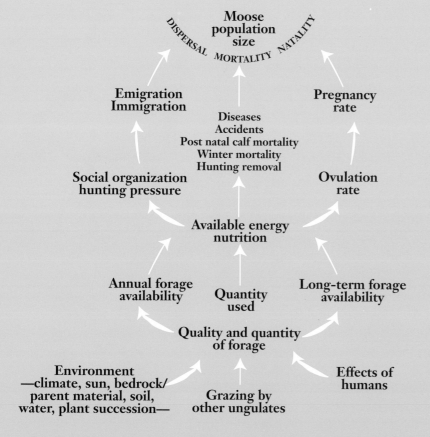

5.5 Probable mechanisms regulating moose population size in Jackson Hole
(after D.B. Houston, 1968, The Shiras moose in Jackson Hole, Wyoming, GTNP Nat. Hist. Soc., Tech. Bull. No. 1)

Canada Geese—Jackson Hole supports about 300 Canada geese year round along the Snake River, but more than twice that number may winter here and breed elsewhere. Additional geese arrive in Jackson Hole in spring to breed. Geese may be observed along Flat Creek just north of Jackson on the National Elk Refuge or along the Snake River in South Park *(figure 5.7)*.

Courtship commences in late February and early March. Nest sites are selected between late March and late May, and nesting begins when snow disappears from the sites. The nests are usually within 50 feet of water, on sandy soils, and near shrubby cover and good feeding areas. Many are built on small islands in the Snake River. Geese actively defend their nests against other geese. About 35 percent of all nests are destroyed by various means, and about three percent are deserted. Ravens and crows are the most serious nest predators.

Breeding pairs constitute about 45 percent of the population. The sex ratio among 333 adults in 1963 was 1.2 males per female. Hatching peaks in late May, and clutches average five eggs. Although gosling mortality appears

5.7 Canada geese

negligible, annual mortality of all geese averages almost 40 percent.

Canada goose population ecology in Jackson Hole is similar to the species' population ecology elsewhere. Like other waterfowl and like elk, mule deer, moose, and martens, geese have

been heavily studied. Unfortunately, the population ecology of the majority of Jackson Hole's species is poorly known.

POPULATION ECOLOGY BASICS

Several principles of population ecology are exemplified by Jackson Hole's elk, mule deer, moose, American martens, Canada geese, and other plant and animal populations. Five basics are examined and illustrated below—distribution, age and sex structure and dynamics, population size and change, population regulation, and population behavior. A sixth population principle—extinction—is discussed separately below.

First, organisms are seldom randomly or evenly distributed throughout their environments. They are usually clustered in some way. Food sources, nest sites, winter range, or social attractions explain the clumping of most animal species. Plants are similarly distributed, not only because individuals of the same species occupy the same habitat, but also because seeds from parent plants tend to fall nearby.

A second principle is that sex and age ratios are good indices of a population's health—whether it is stable, increasing, or decreasing. Wildlife managers recommend hunting seasons based on age and sex data. The sex ratio of most vertebrate populations is about one male to one female (usually written as 1:1) at birth or hatching, but it may differ greatly at various times during the life cycle. For example, blue-winged teal flocks in fall have 1.4 males per female. Each sex is exposed to different mortality factors and therefore is subject to different

mortality rates.

The age structure of populations is especially important in analyzing their dynamics. Just as insurance companies use life-tables to determine survivorship, longevity, and life insurance probabilities, population ecologists arrange age data into life-tables showing age structures, mortality, and longevity. Life-table data can provide clues for follow-up studies on what mortality factors affect what age and sex groups.

A third principle of population ecology is that populations change constantly as new individuals are added through births and immigration and others are lost through death and emigration. Virtually all populations have the capacity for high rates of increase under ideal conditions. This *biotic potential* is seldom realized, however, because many factors restrict rates of increase and stabilize populations at levels found in nature. The factors that limit the biotic potential are collectively called *environmental resistance (figure 5.8)*.

For example, around 1900 few moose were found in Jackson Hole even though climate and vegetation were suitable. After the first few moose immigrated into the valley, the growth rate of this new population was slow simply because the total numbers of

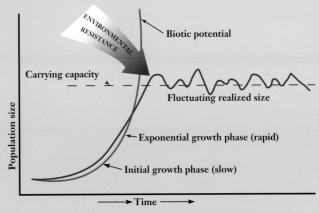

5.8 Environmental resistance places limits on a population's biotic potential

moose were low. But since the habitat was unoccupied, the population subsequently grew exponentially. Eventually, various factors of environmental resistance such as food, space, predation, and disease impeded the growth rate. The population leveled off at its carrying capacity, that is, the maximum population the environment can support for an extended time. Subsequently, the population size fluctuated around the long-term carrying capacity in response to variations in environmental and biological factors.

Nearly all animal populations fluctuate in size seasonally and annually, especially those in temperate climates. Populations usually decline through winter and early spring and increase rapidly during the birth season in late spring and early summer. Infant mortality shortly after birth may then bring about a sharp drop, followed by slowly declining numbers throughout summer and fall. Emigration and immigration generally occur in late winter to spring and fall to early winter.

Some animal populations seem to fluctuate in three- to four-year cycles, including some populations of lemmings, certain field mice, and their predators, such as weasels, snowy owls, and some red foxes. Nine- to ten-year cycles are seen in snowshoe hares and lynx in Canada and less strictly in ruffed grouse, fishers, mink, martens, and muskrats. No theories fully or satisfactorily explain these cycles.

A fourth major principle in population ecology is that the factors regulating population sizes can be classified as either density-independent (also known as environmental or extrinsic factors) or density-dependent (population or intrinsic factors). Density-independent factors operate on all members of a population regardless of its density. For example, a major snowstorm may kill individuals

regardless of how dense the population is. Weather and the availability of food, cover, and space are the major density-independent factors that regulate populations. The effect of density-dependent factors, on the other hand, varies proportionally with changes in population density. As a vole population increases, for instance, weasels can more easily find and prey upon them. Predation will increase until the vole population is so reduced (assuming that no other factors are at work) that the weasels again turn to other prey. In other words, an increase in vole density results in increased predation, and a decrease in density leads to decreased predation. Density-dependent factors largely regulate populations by increasing mortality or decreasing reproductive rates. Predation, disease and parasites, emigration, stress, reproductive rates, and survival of offspring are the main density-dependent regulatory mechanisms.

One of population ecology's major controversies centers on the question of

how populations are regulated. Some ecologists believe that only one class of factors, either density-dependent or density-independent, regulates populations. However, many factors clearly act on populations, and their effects vary in intensity and importance with different species at different times and places. Current thinking is moving away from use of these two terms, and research is focusing on identifying specific regulating mechanisms for specific populations. These species-specific studies are in turn being used to develop theoretical improvements in population ecology.

A fifth principle is that behavior may also play a significant role in regulating population size and density. Even though resources such as space and food may be adequate to support larger numbers of a species in an area, some intrinsic behavioral factors may limit populations to lower numbers and density. Important among these are territoriality and dominance hierarchies.

The Extinction Process

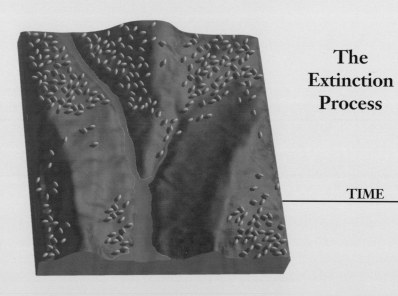

TIME

5.9a The species is abundant, undisturbed, and widely distributed in multiple populations. Management to prevent extinction should begin now before populations are threatened.

Territories are specific areas that are defended against members of the same species. In Jackson Hole male sage grouse establish territories on strutting grounds, or leks, during the breeding season in May. Male blackbirds set up territories on the National Elk Refuge in spring. Coyote packs may also defend areas on the refuge during winter, ensuring access to adequate prey and carrion. By defending territories, an individual or group controls an area and all its resources. Territories are established and maintained by a great variety of behavioral activities and communicative displays. Rarely do animals fight to maintain their territories. Jackson Hole's highly social cliff swallows, for example, exhibit close spacing of nests (about four inches), coordination in nesting activity, and synchrony of reproductive cycles. Nevertheless, frequent displays of intolerance, consisting of threats and fighting, occur at the nesting sites and probably regulate the species' population density.

Dominance hierarchies give socially or physically dominant individuals priority rights over subordinates for resources such as food, mates, cover, and living space. Dominance is usually asserted simply by physically displacing subordinates through threatening displays or, rarely, fighting. Like territoriality, this behavioral mechanism functions to allot resources and regulate population size and density.

POPULATION EXTINCTION

Another principle is that species extinction is caused by a combination of systematic pressures and stochastic (random) events. The process by which populations dwindle to extinction involves many interacting factors and generally recognizable patterns. Knowledge of these can help in conserving species. Although people can intervene to interrupt these patterns and prevent extinction, it is far easier to secure wild populations at

healthy levels than to restore small populations nearing extinction.

Regardless of the initial distribution and abundance of a species, the human-caused *extinction process* proceeds in a typical fashion *(figure 5.9)*. Initially, the species—plant or animal—is abundant, undisturbed, and widely distributed in multiple populations. The first threat is the disruption, modification, or destruction of habitats by human activities *(systematic pressures)*. These may include changes in the natural cycle of fires, for instance, or introducing plowing and logging. Populations may also be reduced by direct threats such as hunting, trapping, poisoning, or collecting. Systematic pressures cause populations of the species to become smaller and increasingly separated from one another. Second, these reduced populations become vulnerable over time to *stochastic (random) events* such as storms (environmental stochasticity), sex ratios

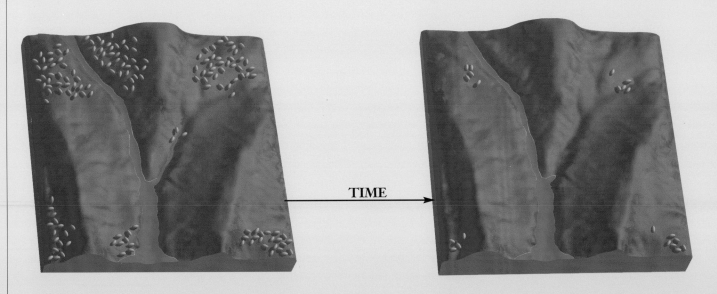

TIME

5.9b *Systematic pressures begin to threaten populations indirectly through habitat disturbance and loss or directly through killing. Populations become increasingly smaller, fragmented, and isolated.*

5.9c *Reduced populations become vulnerable to stochastic events—environmental (fire, drought, disease), demographic (sex ratios, litter sizes), or genetic (genetic drift, inbreeding). Isolated populations become locally extinct. Crisis management is required to save the species.*

5.10 Black-footed ferret

that diverge from 1:1 (demographic stochasticity), and inbreeding or genetic drift (genetic stochasticity). These crises reduce the numbers and sizes of populations even further. Fewer individuals are born and survive and the population gets ever smaller. As isolated populations become locally extinct, the species overall becomes increasingly endangered. Finally, when the last population dwindles to nothing through this process, the species is globally *extinct*.

The extinction process is well known: as populations become smaller, they can become trapped irreversibly in a positive feedback loop toward extinction. Conservation biologists call this downward spiraling process the *extinction vortex*.

Systematic pressures on populations, such as habitat loss through logging, have predictable and deterministic effects. As each acre of forest is cut, a proportionate loss of habitat results. In most cases, populations initially become endangered because of systematic factors. A number of species

in the larger Jackson Hole region illustrate systematic extinction pressures. Wolves were eliminated from Jackson Hole and Greater Yellowstone earlier in this century as a result of intentional, direct killing. Grizzly bears are currently threatened because of overkilling as well as habitat loss and alteration.

After populations have been fragmented and reduced by systematic pressures, stochastic events in their environments, demographics, and genetic makeup are usually the final cause of a population's extinction. A good example of the effect of stochastic events on small populations is the black-footed ferret, a mink-like animal indigenous to North America that preys primarily on prairie dogs *(figure 5.10)*. The last known wild population of ferrets was discovered by chance in 1981 in the mountain basins just east of Yellowstone National Park. All other populations of this species had been exterminated (and this one had been greatly reduced) by humans' systematic killing of prairie dogs (which were believed to compete with crops and livestock). In 1985 a disease epidemic of canine distemper ravaged this remnant population of ferrets at the same time that sylvatic plague hit the prairie dogs—stochastic events. Today that population is extinct! Fortunately, a few surviving ferrets were taken into captivity. The species is slowly being restored through a captive breeding program and release of captive-bred animals to secure habitats in the wild. Concern remains, however, that stochastic genetic factors could yet affect the captive and reintroduced ferrets.

Most species occur naturally as

multiple populations of varying sizes. The wolf, for instance, used to occur over much of North America in essentially one large population. Tweedy's sand verbena, on the other hand, is a naturally rare plant that occurs in only two very small populations in the Greater Yellowstone Ecosystem. Many populations in Jackson Hole are naturally small or are being made so by the encroachment of human activities. Small populations are vulnerable to local extinction. The populations of several species in the Jackson Hole region are formally recognized as endangered, threatened, or sensitive. Among these are the bald eagle, grizzly bear, and wolf. About 124 plants— seven percent of all plants in the Greater Yellowstone Ecosystem—are considered rare and vulnerable. Six fish species, a single reptile species, 20 bird species, and 17 species (25 percent) of mammals in the region are vulnerable. Considerable conservation effort is being expended to improve the status of these species, and in some instances fully developed recovery programs are underway. If a species' need for special conservation attention is recognized by the federal government under the 1973 Endangered Species Act, it may be added to the official list of endangered species. A team of experts may be set up to devise a recovery plan for the species and oversee its implementation. There are a number of special recovery teams active in the region.

Extinction theory has been applied to the American marten population in Jackson Hole. Field research has shown that marten populations are affected by trapping and by logging practices that alter and remove marten habitat. A computer model (appropriately called VORTEX) simulated changes in marten population dynamics in response to various levels of timber harvesting and commercial trapping. The model estimated how likely it was that populations of different initial sizes would become extinct within a given period. The most optimistic scenario—with initial populations of 100 martens, no trapping, no logging, and no immigrants—showed a dismal 66-percent chance of surviving 100 years. Populations of 50 martens rapidly went extinct, especially with logging, trapping, and no immigration. This modeling effort suggested that adequate areas of suitable habitat, corridors between such areas to allow for immigration, and limitations on logging and trapping will be necessary to conserve marten populations of 100 or fewer individuals. Wildlife and forest managers need to be very careful in managing this species and its habitat to ensure that populations persist in Jackson Hole.

RECOMMENDED RESOURCES

Boyce, M. S. 1989. *Elk management in North America: The Jackson herd.* Cambridge University Press, Cambridge. 306 pp.

Campbell, T. M., III. 1991. *Winter ecology of the Gros Ventre Buttes mule deer herd, Jackson Hole, Wyoming:* Winter 1989-1990. Biota Research and Consulting, Jackson, Wyoming. Progress Report XI:1-37 + appendices.

Clark, T. W. 1989. *Conservation biology of the black-footed ferret* Mustela nigripes. Wildlife Preservation Trust Special Scientific Report 3:1-175.

Clark, T. W., T. M. Campbell III, and T. N. Hauptman. 1989b. *Demographic characteristics of American marten population in Jackson Hole, Wyoming.* Great Basin Naturalist 49:587-596.

Clark, T. W., R. M. Warneke, and G. C. George. 1990. *Management and conservation of small populations.* Pp. 1-18 in T. W. Clark, and J. H. Seebeck, eds., Management and conservation of small populations. Chicago Zoological Society, Chicago.

Lacy, R. C., and T. W. Clark. 1993. *Simulation modeling of American marten* (Martes americana) *populations: Vulnerability to extinction.* Great Basin Naturalist 53:282-292.

Schmidt, K. J. 1990. *Conserving Greater Yellowstone: A teacher's guide.* Northern Rockies Conservation Cooperative, Jackson, Wyoming. 232 pp.

Smith, B. L., and R. L. Robbins. 1994. *Migrations and management of the Jackson Hole elk herd.* U.S. Department of Interior, National Biological Survey, Resource Publication 199:1-61.

Biotic Communities

Populations of certain species of plants and animals are often closely associated in a *biotic community*, which is any organized assemblage of populations of organisms inhabiting a specific area or physical habitat. Some biotic communities occur on north slopes, others at certain elevations, and others only under certain moisture conditions. For instance, sage grouse are found together with sagebrush and moose with willows. Associating species on this basis shows how species are interrelated through community processes such as predation and competition and how ecological processes like succession and fire affect species' interactions. The Jackson Hole ecosystem is a dynamic patchwork quilt of biotic communities blanketing the landscape.

CLASSIFICATION OF BIOTIC COMMUNITIES

The science of ecology has brought about increasingly refined schemes for describing and classifying biotic communities based on associations of dominant plants and animals, soils, climate, and elevation. Since Jackson Hole includes Grand Teton National Park and is near Yellowstone National Park, plants have been well collected. By 1976, 921 species of vascular plants had been collected in Teton County. Today the number is closer to 1,100. The animals found in these communities are also well known. Together,

6.1 An aquatic community in Jackson Hole

these assemblages of plants and animals in particular settings make up a diverse set of biotic communities in the valley.

There have been several different schemes for classifying biotic communities. Though not widely used today, the *life-zone* concept of community classification was widely applied in the early days of nature study. A life-zone was characterized by the dominant vegetation at a particular latitude or altitude and by the animals usually associated with it. Another scheme visualized *community complexes* of wholly different plant groups occurring in related patterns. These plant communities were believed to be held together climatically and edaphically (by soil) because of their similar historical origins, but differed in their microclimates and topography.

The classification system used in this book is largely based on the more *dominant plant communities* of Jackson Hole as influenced by geological history, including slope exposure and original glacially-deposited material. The depth of the water table, previous agricultural uses, and other biotic agents (notably beavers) also affect sites and vegetation.

BIOTIC COMMUNITIES OF JACKSON HOLE

Ecologists generally recognize at least 11 major biotic communities in the valley that are sufficiently large and complete to be relatively independent. Somewhat different schemes are used

by Don Despain in his book, *Yellowstone vegetation: Consequences of environment and history in a natural setting* (1990), and by Dennis Knight in his book, *Mountains and plains: The ecology of Wyoming landscapes* (1994). A popular book by Frank Craighead, *For everything there is a season* (1994), documents the *phenology*, or sequence of natural events in communities, in the Grand Teton-Yellowstone area. These excellent accounts bring much additional detail to the following descriptions of biotic communities in Jackson Hole.

Aquatic—The aquatic community, found in ponds (including those dammed by beavers), small streams, and backwaters of the Snake River, is distinguished by plants that grow under, on, or above the water surface *(figure 6.1)*. Adjacent to the water, there are numerous muddy stream banks and mud-covered depressions, limited in extent, that are sporadically flooded. Growing in these areas are "amphibious" plant species and terrestrial pioneers. Sod forms near the edge of quiet water where neither active erosion nor deposition occurs; such areas are characterized by sedges, rushes, grasses, and forbs. Shifting stream channels expose new areas that are vegetated by rushes, horsetails, forbs, and, ultimately, willows and some trees.

Fish, amphibians, and several reptiles are associated with these communities. Jackson Hole also has diverse waterfowl and shorebirds that use these areas. Numerous aquatic invertebrates found here become food for fish and amphibians. Beavers, muskrats, and river otters also frequent aquatic communities.

Cottonwood—Cottonwood trees grow along stream and river sides, usually on terraces slightly above normal flood level, thoughout Jackson Hole. In established streamside forests, clumps of blue spruce are found amongst the narrow-leaf and other cottonwoods. Willows, buffaloberries, roses, and honeysuckles may be part of the understory, along with forbs, wildflowers, and grasses. At the edges furthest from the water, the cottonwood community usually ends abruptly as it meets sagebrush, aspen, or lodgepole communities. Somewhat higher terraces may be dominated by grasses and wildflowers.

This community includes both terrestrial and some semi-aquatic animal species, such as long-tailed weasels, mink, and beavers. Bald eagles and osprey nest here.

Meadow—Jackson Hole's meadow community is underlain by very firm sod and is often covered for long periods during the growing season by standing water a few inches deep. Wetter parts of this community are dominated by sedges with some grasses and forbs. Meadows are also found on more elevated, drier sites where sedges and grasses co-dominate. Forbs are also found here, particularly clovers. This highly productive community covers much of the southern end of the National Elk Refuge *(figure 6.2)*.

The meadow community is rich in vertebrate species. Voles are common and numerous birds are also found.

Willow—Willows are abundant where the water table is very near the soil surface and previous vegetation has stabilized the soil *(figure 6.3)*. At least 20 species of willow occur in Jackson Hole, including Bebb's, blueberry, Geyer's, interior, Scouler's, whiplash, Wolf's, and yellow willow. Many of these species hybridize and make positive identifica-

tion difficult. Other shrubs may be found here, along with grassy areas and wooded areas of cottonwoods or scattered clumps of Engelmann and blue spruce. The relatively closed canopy formed by willows combined with abundant moisture and deep, rich soils favors an abundant and vigorous growth of many forbs and grasses. Over 60 plant species are present.

A large bird and mammal fauna may be present in the willow community. Common birds are yellow warbler, MacGillivray's warbler, common yellowthroat, Wilson's warbler, Lincoln's sparrow, song sparrow, and willow flycatcher. Common mammals are mountain voles, long-tailed voles, red-backed voles, Richardson's voles, water shrews, wandering and masked shrews, jumping mice, gophers, and white-footed deer mice. Beavers and muskrats are also common. Moose frequent the willow community, especially during winter when willows are critical habitat for them and may support over 40 moose per square mile.

6.2 *The meadow community*

6.3 *The willow community*

6.4 The sagebrush community dominates the floor of Jackson Hole. Here a small herd of mule deer browses.

Moose use the willow community 75 percent of the time in late winter.

Sagebrush—This is the most widespread and conspicuous plant community in Jackson Hole *(figure 6.4)*. At first glance, it appears to be a relatively simple community of sagebrush, a few forbs, and grasses. But in fact it is one of the most complex, containing over 100 plant species and providing habitat for numerous animal species.

This community occurs primarily on the coarse-textured soils of the glacial outwash plains on the valley floor and on till-covered hillsides. Three shrubs are common—big sagebrush, low sagebrush, and antelope bitterbrush. Low sagebrush dominates west of the Snake River and big sagebrush east of the Snake, except where antelope bitterbrush co-dominates with big sagebrush near Blacktail Butte. These dominant shrubs probably are distributed in response to soil moisture, soil aeration, and the depth that roots can penetrate.

Other shrubs are scattered throughout the sagebrush community, including threetip sagebrush, serviceberry, Oregon grape, and snowberry. Over 20 grass species grow beneath the shrubs; foremost are wheat grasses and brome grasses, Idaho fescue, junegrass, bluegrass, and needlegrass. In addition, over 100 species of forbs grow in this community.

Numerous birds and animals live in the sagebrush community. Herbivores include Uinta ground squirrels, white-footed deer mice, a few least chipmunks, and an occasional white-tailed jackrabbit. Badgers may be present. Areas where antelope bitterbrush co-dominates with sagebrush are heavily used by pronghorn and moose. Some common birds are sage grouse, sage thrashers, western meadowlarks, green-tailed towhees, vesper sparrows, and Brewer's sparrows. Raptors include Swainson's and red-tailed hawks, American kestrels, prairie falcons, northern harriers, and golden eagles. On summer nights, bats and nighthawks commonly feed on insects.

Sagebrush is readily killed by fires. A three-acre parcel can be seen just east of Blacktail Butte that burned in 1974, and there are more extensive recent burns on Burro Hill, near Uhl Draw, and near Mormon Row. When the shrubs are burned, nutrients are released into the soil, competition for soil moisture is reduced, and herbaceous plants grow rapidly. Once a heavy grass and forb layer is established, sagebrush is slow to reinvade. Sagebrush has generally increased in Jackson Hole during the last 100 years primarily because of fire suppression. Population

6.5 The aspen community

declines of birds and mammals following sagebrush fires are short lived. Within only three years after a fire, animal populations almost reach preburn levels.

Aspen—The silver-white bark and golden autumn leaves of aspen make this community a prominent one. Aspens grow 30 to 60 feet tall and one to two feet in diameter. In Jackson Hole two distinct aspen-dominated communities exist—relatively open stands on dry hillsides with less developed soils and relatively dense stands on flatter terrain where soil is deeper, moister, and richer in organic matter *(figure 6.5).*

Species diversity differs in the two aspen-dominated communities. Only 38 species of vascular plants, including four shrubs, have been found in the dry, hillside community, while 78 species, including 11 shrubs, have been found in lowland communities. More than twice as many forbs and grasses occur in moist aspen stands as in dry stands.

Aspen stands are excellent places to watch birds, especially in late spring. Numerous species nest and feed there. Ruffed grouse drumming on downed logs—a courtship display—are easily observed in May. Other common species are red-shafted flicker, tree swallow, yellow-bellied sapsucker, downy woodpecker, black-capped and mountain chickadees, white-breasted nuthatch, house wren, robin, dusky flycatcher, mountain bluebird, Townsend's solitaire, ruby-crowned kinglet, and numerous others.

Few mammals live in the tree canopy, although several species occupy lower vegetation layers, including the jumping mouse, masked and wandering shrews, meadow vole, mountain vole, long-tailed vole, and white-footed deer mice.

Fire plays an important role in maintaining the aspen community. Within the last several decades, mature aspen stands in Jackson Hole have deteriorated considerably. Until recently, this degradation was attributed to overuse by elk, which were thought to be more numerous than in pristine times. Recent evidence, however, shows that elk are less numerous now and that aspen decline is largely the result of alteration of the natural fire regime to which aspens are adapted. Fire that kills mature aspen trees apparently stimulates aspen roots to send up many new stems or suckers.

Aspen trees rarely exceed 200 years in age, and an aspen stand commonly begins to deteriorate at about 80 years. Without periodic fires, the pressures of heavy browsing, disease, and increased competition with conifers will kill entire stands. Most aspen stands in the Gros Ventre River-Spread Creek area were established following fires between 1840 and 1890, but very little reproduction has occurred since 1900 because of fire suppression. As a result, many stands are 100 years or older and are deteriorating rapidly. If fire does not occur in the next few decades, the extent of aspen in Jackson Hole will likely be greatly reduced. As a result, the U.S. Forest Service is carrying out a program of prescribed fires to restore this community.

Lodgepole Pine—Three major coniferous (evergreen) communities occur in Jackson Hole—lodgepole pine, Douglas fir, and spruce-fir. In addition, there is a limited distribution of juniper. The key in *figure 6.6* will help identify all the native conifers in Jackson Hole.

Lodgepole pine is the most conspicuous tree community to most visitors to the valley *(figure 6.7)*. It is so extensive that it forms a continuous forest from the foothills of the Absaroka Range in eastern Yellowstone and the southern shores of Yellowstone Lake across the rolling hills of Bridger-Teton National Forest to the south flank of the Teton Range. It is largely confined to well-drained, sandy soils on the valley floor and on lower mountain slopes with a variety of soils where it grows in almost pure stands. It is a straight and slender tree usually 70 to 80 feet tall. Its leaves are two-to-three inch-long needles in clusters of two. Cones are usually one to two inches long. Undisturbed stands may take nearly 100 to 200 years to reach maturity. Individual trees may exceed 300 years in age.

The lodgepole pine community seems to be increasing in extent and spreading south in Jackson Hole, as evidenced by the many young trees growing alone and sometimes in clumps in the sagebrush community east and south of Signal Mountain. Periods of relatively high moisture have permitted a few lodgepole trees to become established in sagebrush meadows.

This species regenerates well following fire. In fact, it sometimes produces serotinous cones that will not open and shed their seeds unless heated above 112° F. Following a fire, many lodgepole seedlings spring up and produce a very dense, even-aged stand. Such dense stands are usually devoid not only of herbaceous understory plants but also soil stratification and birds. Overall the lodgepole pine community is perpetuated by fire, and typically succession moves it toward a spruce-fir community. (Spruce and fir seedlings thrive in the shade of mature

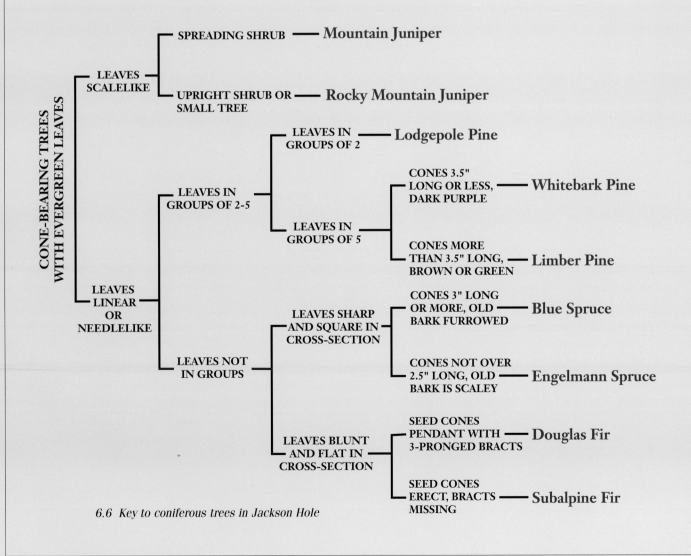

6.6 *Key to coniferous trees in Jackson Hole*

6.7 Lodgepole pine community

lodgepole forests, but if the forest burns, only the lodgepole seedlings will thrive in the absence of canopy shade.)

Since lodgepole pines are shallow rooted and often grow in sandy soils, they are subject to windfalls. Windfalls greatly add to ground fuels and fires readily burn these windfall areas. Lodgepole pine windfalls may be seen west of Cottonwood Creek. The Jenny Lake campground is in a lodgepole pine forest that blew down in 1973.

Because of the relatively poor soil and short growing season, the rate at which the lodgepole pine community develops and is succeeded by the spruce-fir community is very slow. Normally, lodgepole pine stands are 100 to 200 years old before any appreciable numbers of spruce and fir seedlings appear. However, lodgepole pines become susceptible to attack by mountain pine beetles when they reach 80 to 100 years old. Fire suppression has allowed many stands in Jackson Hole to reach this age, and thus a much larger area of the lodgepole pine community has become susceptible to

beetle attack than when natural fire kept more area in younger, less susceptible stands. In Grand Teton National Park and Bridger-Teton National Forest, most lodgepole pine stands recently have become vulnerable to beetle attacks. Ten to 45 percent of lodgepole pine over five inches in diameter were killed from 1960 to 1972.

The variation within the lodgepole pine community—from even-aged stands where trees are "dog-hair" thick to old stands that are thinning out— provides a range of habitats for many animals. Elk, mule deer, red squirrels, flying squirrels, yellow pine chipmunks, pocket gophers, white-footed deer mice, red-backed voles, snowshoe hares, black and grizzly bears, martens, and masked and wandering shrews are present. Birds include goshawk, ruffed grouse, great gray owl, hairy woodpecker, Steller's and gray jays, Clark's nutcracker, brown creeper, Cassin's finch, pine grosbeak, pine siskin, dark-eyed junco, red crossbill, and others.

Douglas Fir—Douglas fir may occur in dense or open stands. The

smooth, gray-brown bark on young trees becomes thick, dark, and deeply furrowed on older trunks *(figure 6.8)*. Douglas fir trees may reach 400 to 600 years of age and four to five feet in diameter.

In Jackson Hole Douglas fir often occurs on dry, warm, south- and east-facing slopes up to about 8,000 feet, but pure stands are also found on the north side of Blacktail Butte and the west slopes of Sheep Mountain, for example. This tree frequently grows on ridge tops and wind-swept, dry sites within other forest communities, such as along the Hoback River. On the warmest and driest sites, such as some south-facing slopes in the Gros Ventre Mountains, it may occur with limber pine. Relatively large stands occur in eastern Jackson Hole at lower elevations. In northern parts of the valley, Douglas fir occurs on sites that are unsuitable for the establishment of other tree species, such as ridges, shallow swales, and south-facing slopes.

Disturbances, including fire, tend to perpetuate Douglas fir communities for several hundred years. Open stands of Douglas fir are very resistant to damage from fires. Thick bark protects the trees from ground fires, and the openness of the stands makes crown fires infrequent. Ground fires also burn out competing shrubs and young trees. In dense stands of Douglas firs, such as on Blacktail Butte, however, crown fires could kill many trees.

A large fire swept Blacktail Butte in 1879, leaving only the largest Douglas firs. Subsequent suppression of fires has resulted in considerable build-up of fuel from fallen trees, and despite current fire suppression efforts, Blacktail Butte will eventually burn again. If no minor fires occur there for another 50 to 100 years, a major fire could destroy all the Douglas firs. Since aspen and willow

6.8 Solitary Douglas fir tree

6.9 Spruce-fir community on a hillside

have deteriorated greatly on Blacktail Butte, development of a new forest community could be very slow.

Birds seen in the Douglas fir community include ruffed grouse, yellow-bellied sapsucker, black-capped and mountain chickadees, white-breasted and red-breasted nuthatches, golden-crowned kinglet, western tanager, black-headed grosbeak, Cassin's finch, pine siskin, dark-eyed junco, and chipping sparrow. Predatory birds include the great horned owl, Cooper's and sharp-shinned hawks, and goshawk.

Tree cover in this community is used by elk and mule deer. Red squirrels are common. If Douglas fir is associated with rocky outcrops, yellow-bellied marmots and golden-mantled ground squirrels are abundant. Red-backed voles, white-footed deer mice, pocket gophers, and bushy-tailed woodrats may be common.

Spruce-Fir—Engelmann spruce and subalpine fir are the dominant trees in this community, which is generally

found at higher elevations and on cold, wet, north-facing slopes at lower elevations *(figure 6.9)*. At high elevations white-barked pine may also be present. The abundance of Engelmann spruce and subalpine fir near Teton Pass indicates that this is a "cloud-milking" area. Moisture-bearing winds from the south and west release their precipitation here as they rise over the Teton Range. This phenomenon accounts for the dryness of Jackson Hole and Gros Ventre Mountains, which are in the rain shadow of the Teton Range.

Engelmann spruce may grow in a savannah-like mosaic of meadows and clumps of trees, but it also occurs in dense stands with a characteristic understory of herbaceous plants, many of which are usually not found elsewhere. Engelmann spruce is also easily killed by fire, and establishment after a fire is slow. Subalpine fir would eventually replace Engelmann spruce in Jackson Hole in the prolonged absence of fire. This species is uncommon in lodgepole pine forests on the valley

floor in Grand Teton National Park, partly because of fires in the late 1800s that eliminated seed sources.

Subalpine fir has increased greatly because of fire suppression in recent decades. It is usually the main tree species to invade lodgepole pine communities in the successional sequence of Jackson Hole. It is easily destroyed by fire, but if individuals survive near a burned area, the subalpine fir readily re-establishes itself. A dense young lodgepole pine stand usually has few firs in it, but within 80 to 100 years and in the absence of fire, the shade-tolerant fir seedlings become established. They will replace the pines within 250 to 400 years.

Because of low temperatures and deep snow cover, the spruce-fir community harbors few animal populations during winter, but populations are relatively large during summer. The exception to this is the small mammal populations, which persist even under deep snows. Moose are year round residents. Subalpine fir is a major moose food during the winter. The increase in subalpine fir may be an important reason for the marked increase of moose in Jackson Hole since 1900.

Other mammals that use this community seasonally include elk, mule deer, Uinta chipmunk, American marten, porcupine, long-tailed weasel, wolverine, mountain lion, snowshoe hare, and an abundant small mammal fauna. Birds found here include blue grouse, Williamson's sapsucker, hairy woodpecker, great gray owl, Hammond's and olive-sided flycatcher, cordilleran flycatcher, gray jay, Steller's jay, raven, Clark's nutcracker, mountain chickadee, red-breasted nuthatch, red crossbill, and others.

Juniper—Rocky Mountain juniper, the dominant tree in this community, is common on some dry south-facing slopes of the buttes in the south central part of the valley and along the Gros Ventre River. Several shrubs, grasses, and forbs grow in this community.

Relatively few vertebrates occur here. There are least chipmunks and marmots in the rocky outcrop areas, and mule deer may winter in these areas.

Alpine Tundra—This community

Yellow-bellied marmots

extends from the upper limit of trees to the tops of the highest mountains *(figure 6.10)*. Vegetation is mostly herbaceous with a few low or dwarf shrubs. The climate of these mountain summits is very cool and moist, and soil is rather scant. On the most severe sites, large angular boulders, which represent the first stage in the change from rock to soil, may be strewn over the landscape. Vegetation in these boulder fields is chiefly crustose lichens growing on the surfaces of the boulders. In less rigorous habitats, coarse gravelly soil has accumulated between the boulders, and on these fell fields, vegetation is sparse and usually includes phlox and pussytoes. In even more favorable habitats, especially at lower elevations near timberline, the boulders have been reduced to soil and the vegetation is a mat of dense, low plants. The

alpine tundra is dominated by sedges, grasses, and shrubs.

Birds and mammals in the tundra community mostly leave or hibernate during winter. Common summer birds are the golden eagle, horned lark, white-crowned sparrow, black-rosy finch, water pipit, raven, and Clark's nutcracker. The Uinta chipmunk, golden-mantled ground squirrel, yellow-bellied marmot, and pika are usually common.

BIOTIC COMMUNITY BASICS
Structure and Dynamics—Communities should be visualized in terms of all their plants and animals and the interactions among these organisms. *Community structure* refers to the physical components and their spatial organization, while *community dynamics* is the interactions, energetic relation-

6.10 Sketch from atop Rendezvous Mountain of the alpine tundra

CANOPY ZONE
(MATURE TREES)

INTERMEDIATE ZONE
(TREE SAPLINGS)

SHRUB ZONE
HERBACEOUS GROUND ZONE

A. TOPSOIL

B. SUBSOIL

C. PARENT MATERIAL

SOIL HORIZON

6.11 Soil and plant strata in a spruce-fir community in Jackson Hole

ships, and patterns of change within communities. Let us examine the structure of a spruce-fir community *(figure 6.11)*. It has a layered structure with characteristic plant and animal populations in each layer.

Soil is the structural foundation of most terrestrial communities. It is a water purifier, a reservoir, and a food bank of chemical nutrients. The mineral and organic composition, texture, and profile characteristics of the soil obviously have a major influence on the plant and animal communities living within it—and vice versa. Burrowing animals like the pocket gophers and ground squirrels in Jackson Hole play a vital role in the aeration, cultivation, and hydration of soil and in the decomposition of organic matter.

Above the soil is a layer dominated by herbs and forbs—the *herbaceous ground zone*. Insects, birds, and small mammals live at this level. Larger mammals such as the snowshoe hare, red fox, coyote, striped skunk, marten, and long-tailed weasel may also be present.

The next layer of larger shrubs, tree seedlings, and saplings—the *shrub zone*—also has characteristic animals, mostly insects and birds, but elk and mule deer may have a major influence on it. A few mammals such as the red squirrel and porcupine are present although they also use higher and lower layers. Stratification is most evident for birds. Although birds are obviously capable of ranging from forest floor to tree tops, they show definite preferences for certain layers.

Above that is the *intermediate zone* made up of tree saplings. Depending on community type, tree saplings may be widely spaced or so dense that it is impossible to walk through them (such as lodgepole pine stands following fires). There is usually severe competition for light by tree saplings with each other and with older, larger trees. Some tree sapling species are used as food by ungulates and nesting habitat for birds.

The *canopy zone* of mature, overstory trees dominates forested biotic communities. These highest levels of tree growth capture sunlight, influence how much moisture falls to lower

levels, and, in turn, affect many aspects of plant and animal distribution and abundance in forests.

Community structure is often described in terms of *species diversity*. This is most simply expressed as the number of species in a community, but more informatively expressed as the numbers of species, the number of individuals of each species, and the total number of individuals of all species in that community. Ecologists have devised several sophisticated ways to measure and express species diversity and make comparisons among biotic communities.

Why has natural selection produced such a great diversity of living organisms—several thousand plant and animal species in Jackson Hole alone and over twenty million in the world? In part, the infinitely variable environmental conditions that cover the landscape have allowed the evolution of distinct plant communities (both major and minor) with associated animal species, each adapted to a specific set of environmental conditions. The addition of each new plant and animal species to a community increases its diversity, thus creating a new set of conditions on which evolution will operate.

A rough correlation is thought to exist between species diversity and *community stability*. Biotic communities with greater species diversity have more complexly intertwined food webs. That is, each species has several alternatives for meeting its life requirements, and this cushions them against ecological upsets in the community. Major change in a plant or animal population in the relatively non-diverse tundra community will likely have a far greater impact on the total community than a similar change in the more diverse lowland aspen community. Obviously, communities with simpler structure and dynamics are more susceptible and vulnerable to ecological upset—including impacts by humans.

The ultimate factor that limits biological diversity is the physical environment. Environments with the harshest and most variable conditions have communities with the lowest species diversity (for example, the tundra). Communities in milder and less variable environments have the greatest species diversity (meadows, shrub-swamp, and lowland aspen, for example).

A relatively few species exert a major controlling influence on a community by virtue of their numbers, size, production, or other influences. These organisms are called *ecological dominants.* Many of the biotic communities are named after dominant species, including willow, aspen, and lodgepole pine.

Niche Theory—All organisms have a *habitat*, the place where they live, and a *niche*, a functional role in the biotic community. The niche of an organism is the physical and functional "space" in which it lives and reproduces. A niche can be described by measuring all the resources required for the species' survival. The concept of niche is closely tied to competition among species, or *interspecific competition.* Interrelationships among species greatly influence the type and size of an organism's niche.

An organism's *fundamental niche* is the idealized or theoretical niche comprising all the factors required for survival in the absence of competitors—food size or availability, foraging location, humidity, photoperiod, temperature range, mineral and vitamin requirements, and others. An organism's *realized niche* is made up of the conditions under which the organism actually exists and includes the impacts

of competitors. A realized niche is nearly always smaller than a fundamental niche.

Niche overlap occurs when two or more organisms or species use the same resource at the same time. If the resource is in short supply, competition results. Niche overlap is proportional to the degree of competition—the more the overlap, the more the competition. For example, many of the meadow mice or voles in Jackson Hole are physically similar, occur in the same habitat type, and are probably under severe competition with one another at certain times for food and cover. A species' niche may be narrow or wide relative to other species. Species with broad niches are generalists; those with narrow niches are specialized. For example, the common deer mouse, which lives in a wide variety of communities and eats many different foods, has a very broad niche. The water shrew, on the other hand, occurs only in certain aquatic communities and consumes a limited number of food items and thus has a very narrow niche. Niche width changes over time, contracting or expanding depending on other species in the community.

Interspecies Relationships— Some species are directly linked by their activities to other species in the community. These interactions take many forms.

Competition denotes the simultaneous use of limited resources by two or more species. There are many mechanisms for successful competition, including aggression, higher reproductive rates, increased survivorship through better disease resistance, more successful food finding and consumption, and more efficient use of energy and materials. The Competitive Exclusion Principle says that competition tends to bring about the ecological

separation of closely related or otherwise similar species. The chipmunks of Jackson Hole have probably undergone competitive exclusion in their evolutionary history that has resulted in a certain amount of separation: the Uinta chipmunk occupies open areas at high elevations, the least chipmunk is more broadly distributed at lower elevations in sagebrush, Douglas fir, and some other communities, and the yellow pine chipmunk lives in the lodgepole pine community.

Parasitism is another kind of interspecific relationship in which one organism uses a host organism for food with negative but usually not fatal effects on the host. Round and flatworms, for instance, are gut parasites in many mammals. In *mutualism* both species benefit; lichens covering many rocks and trees are made up of a fungus and an algae. In *commensalism*, one species is benefited while the other is unaffected. Certain zoöplankton (very small aquatic animals), for example, benefit from living in association with fresh water sponges, whereas the sponges remain unaffected by the association.

Predation is the killing and eating of one animal species by another. In the Jackson Hole ecosystem, predators range from microscopic animals to grizzly bears. There are thousands of small predators, but only the few that interfere or compete with human activities attract any attention or arouse animosity. Many predators are wholly beneficial to humans, such as bats, swallows, and bluebirds.

The diets of most predators are as varied as those of most humans. Hawks, eagles, and owls prey on mice, rats, squirrels, gophers, rabbits, fish, and birds. Snakes and lizards eat frogs, fish, toads, eggs, rodents, insects, and young birds. Predators such as badgers, foxes, and coyotes feed on squirrels, marmots, rabbits, mice, fish, frogs, and larger species like wolves and bears sometimes take larger prey such as elk and deer. Most predators are opportunists—they take what is most readily available, including some plant material. Predators often kill animals that would otherwise die from starvation, disease, freezing, or parasites.

Predator control is believed by some people to be a sure method of increasing game abundance; advocates of control think that predators rob them of game. However, numerous investigations on a wide variety of predator-prey systems have shown that predator control will usually not increase the game supply unless predation is the major factor limiting game populations. These studies show that predators are seldom the limiting factor. Coyotes have been subject of predation and behavior studies in Jackson Hole. Coyote predation is not the limiting factor for any species thus far studied in the valley. With wolves returning to Jackson Hole, their predation will have an effect on elk, deer, and other species, but it is unlikely that it will be a controlling factor.

SUCCESSION

The biotic communities in Jackson Hole did not spring full-blown into their present forms. When glaciers retreated from Jackson Hole 10,000 years ago, parts of the valley had been scoured down to bedrock. The communities present today developed slowly over the centuries, beginning when pioneer species invaded these newly exposed and barren areas. As less harsh environments and better soils developed, these pioneers were slowly replaced by a more diverse array of other species. This replacement of one community by another in an orderly and predictable way over time is called *ecological succession*. Succession is usually a plant-driven or plant-dominated process. Animal communities follow and change as plants change.

Ecological succession ends with the development of complex *climax communities*, which are stable and self-perpetuating as long as they are not severely disturbed. There are three theoretical approaches to the climax concept. The *monoclimax theory* recognizes only a single climax in any area, the characteristics of which are determined by the climate. The *polyclimax theory* says that the climax community of a region is made up of a mosaic of different vegetation types, each controlled by soil nutrients and mois-

ture, topography, slope, exposure, fire, and animal activity. The *climax pattern theory* says that an ecosystem's entire environment determines the composition of the climax community and that the climax community is the one that is most widespread and prevailing at any given time.

Like other communities, the climax community stores nutrients and energy in a diversity of plants and animals that represent the culmination of hundreds and sometimes thousands of years of succession. Because of natural disturbances such as fire, flooding, and droughts, no place on earth supports a climax community forever, and climax communities change in response to long-term climatic change. Within Jackson Hole there is constant change: communities in some areas are at or near the climax while others are progressing or retrogressing through various stages of succession. Thus a complex and very dynamic mosaic of communities covers the landscape and provides diverse environments for many plants and animals. Some changes that occur during succession are shown in *figure 6.12*.

There are two types of succession. *Primary succession* occurs in areas previously unoccupied by living organisms. In Jackson Hole such barren land includes areas exposed by retreating glaciers or by landslides. Here it takes a very long time—commonly several thousand years—to reach the climax stage. Examples of primary succession can be seen along the retreating edges of glaciers in the Teton Range and on the Gros Ventre Slide. Primary succession also takes place on lands once covered by water: Open water gives way to submerged and then emergent vegetation. As the ground becomes stabilized, sedges and rushes follow, then grasses, herbs, and forbs dominate,

FACTORS ⟶ Changes over successional time

BARE ROCK ⟶	Broken down and weathered
SOILS ⟶	Progressively develop, deepen, and differentiate into layers
PLANTS ⟶	Increase in height and massiveness, differentiate into strata
PRODUCTIVITY ⟶	Formation of organic mater per unit area increases
MICROCLIMATE ⟶	More and more determined by the vegetation
SPECIES DIVERSITY ⟶	Increases
SPECIES ⟶	Smaller, short-lived species are replaced by larger, longer-lived species
STABILITY ⟶	Increases

6.12 Some trends in ecological succession in Jackson Hole

and finally succession advances to shrubs and trees. This sequence can be seen in the pothole lakes and ponds south of Jackson Lake. The more common *secondary succession* occurs on sites where previous biotic communities have been altered by some disturbance, such as fire. Secondary succession to climax may take 50 to 200 years.

Although ecological succession may seem to be a simple linear process leading to a single climax community everywhere in Jackson Hole, this is not the case. Some *seral* (developmental) stages below climax may persist for hundreds or thousands of years in dynamic equilibrium with varying environmental factors, including slope exposure and parent material (original rock substrate), moisture, wind, and elevation. For instance, the sagebrush community on south-facing slopes where soil is thin will probably persist as long as the climate does not change dramatically. If the climate becomes wetter, however, succession would proceed towards climax spruce-fir.

Fire Ecology—The last three decades have seen several fires in Jackson Hole and larger ones in the Greater Yellowstone Ecosystem *(figure 6.13)*. Recent research has provided abundant evidence of the major role of fire in shaping the biotic communities present today in the valley. Dates obtained from growth rings in fire-scarred trees and weather records since 1916 indicate that conditions conducive to severe fires—dryness, lightning, and high winds—occur rarely. The highest potential for fire occurs between July 15 and September 30, but burning conditions vary greatly from summer to summer. The numerous fire-scarred, living trees throughout Jackson Hole provide evidence of frequent creeping ground fires that consumed fuels such as herbs, shrubs, downed trees, and organic litter but only occasionally ignited tree crowns. Crown fires that burn through treetops occur only in dry, windy weather.

Prior to effective fire suppression beginning around 1900, most natural fires were probably small, although they might persist for months. Large fires were rare because conditions that favored them were rare and because the rugged mountains provided numerous natural fire breaks. However, these rare but widespread and often intense fires probably had the greatest influence on biotic communities of Jackson Hole. Large fires occurred about 1765, in the early 1840s, about 1856, and off and on from 1878 through 1898. Most of the forest communities in the valley today developed following fires in 1856 and 1879. Fires burned somewhere in the Gros Ventre River drainage each decade of the nineteenth century, the largest about 1842, 1872, and 1879. Dates obtained from fire-scarred Douglas firs 300 to 400 years old indicate that numerous fires also occurred in the 1600s and 1700s. In 1897 large tracts of timber of merchantable size were rare because recurring fires had left no areas unburned and had reburned some areas repeatedly within a generation.

Ecological succession in the absence of fire has resulted in older-aged and more extensive coniferous forest communities, deterioration of aspen communities, and an increase of some shrub communities, especially big sagebrush, in place of herbaceous communities. Fire suppression has produced a more homogeneous ecosystem by eliminating communities created and maintained by fire. This more homogeneous ecosystem consequently supports fewer wildlife species.

Although fires may appear destructive to wildlife, animal populations have evolved with fire as a major component of their environments. Most wildlife species are benefited by periodic fires. Lack of fires has resulted in a decline in the number of animals that Bridger-Teton National Forest can support, although wildlife is still abundant there. The beaver is one of the majority of wildlife species adversely affected by fire suppression. Aspen and willow, which provide food and lodge- and dam-building materials, have declined in abundance in Jackson Hole because of fire suppression. As a consequence, beaver have also declined. Ruffed grouse are also detrimentally affected by fire suppression, which prevents the renewal or regeneration of early successional stages needed by grouse. Habitat improvement efforts for such species must be directed toward rejuvenation and diversification of the vegetation. Fire is the only practical tool available to do this.

There are some exceptions to this trend toward reduced carrying capacity with advancing succession. Some species exist only in late succession or climax communities. Carrying capacity increases for cavity-nesting birds such as woodpeckers when aspen stands deteriorate, for moose when subalpine fir increases, and for mule deer when sagebrush and other shrubs increase on winter range—all of which happen when fires do not occur.

The advertisement to "prevent forest fires" that shows a fire raging toward a nest of baby birds and claims that "fires burn more than trees" is misleading. Not only have most birds finished nesting long before most forest fires occur in late summer and fall, but forest fires can be advantageous to certain bird species by initiating the *tree-hole nesting cycle*. In this cycle, many burned trees remain standing, some for 30 or 40 years, following a severe forest

6.13 *Fire in Grand Teton National Park.*

suppression to a more flexible fire management program. To restore fire to the ecosystem, it was recommended that the national forest be subdivided into fire management zones. Strict fire suppression would continue in valuable timber stands, recreational areas, and developed areas. Fires would be allowed to burn within predetermined limits in other areas, including wildlife habitats and wilderness areas. Prescribed (human-controlled) burns would be conducted where vegetation needed to be returned to an earlier successional stage to improve livestock grazing and elk habitat, for instance, where sagebrush had invaded grasslands, or where aspen was deteriorating.

Grand Teton National Park's fire-vegetation management plan divides the park into four fire management zones. In Zone I all naturally-caused fires will be allowed to burn except where human life is endangered or where fire could spread to other zones. All human-caused fires will be extinguished. In Zone II natural fires may be allowed to burn depending on fire-hazard conditions, and some prescribed burns may be carried out. All fires in Zone III will be extinguished unless they can be managed as prescribed, controlled burns. Developed areas, Zone IV, will be manipulated by logging, planting, or other methods to maintain desired landscapes.

The large fires in the Greater Yellowstone Ecosystem in 1988 spawned wide public interest in fires. Numerous books, news stories, films, and videos depicted and described the force of the fires, the role of fire in ecosystems, the effects of fire on plants and animals, and the debate about fire policy and management. Many lessons have been drawn from the 1988 fires for improved fire policy and management, including the fact that fires are

fire. Because of the egg-laying insects that live in them, these trees are favored by insectivorous birds such as black-backed and three-toed woodpeckers, which are uncommon in unburned forests in Jackson Hole. The woodpeckers feed on beetle larvae and peck nest chambers in the burned trees. These species decrease the second year after a fire because their favored beetle larvae decrease, to be replaced by other

less preferred insects. But hairy woodpeckers increase in this period for the reverse reason. Mountain bluebirds, tree swallows, nuthatches, and chickadees subsequently nest in abandoned woodpecker holes for many years.

Fire is a natural agent responsible for the periodic renewal of the Jackson Hole vegetative mosaic. Recent studies on Bridger-Teton National Forest resulted in a shift from strict fire generally beneficial to a region's ecology and that the public needs to be informed about this positive role.

Paleoecology of Northwestern Wyoming—Studies of *paleoecology* (prehistoric ecology) in Grand Teton and Yellowstone National Parks in the last 25 years provide glimpses of changes in climate and vegetation spanning millions of years, although the record has been obscured by repeated volcanic activity and glaciation. Fossilized evidence of more than 100 plant species including 10 forms of cycads, three horsetails, 10 conifers (including redwoods), and 76 flowering plants have been found in both parks. Most of the better fossils are from the Eocene epoch (58 to 36 million years ago).

Climatic conditions during the Eocene are thought to have been similar to those found today in southeastern and south central United States—warm to subtropical with 50 to 60 inches of rain per year. The region was only about 3,000 feet above sea level. Tree species included hardwoods such as maple, magnolia, and sycamore. The subtropical climate changed to the present cool-temperate-subarctic climate with uplifting of the entire Rocky Mountain region by nearly 7,000 feet during the last 36 million years. During the Ice Age (last one million years), a few mountain peaks escaped being covered by ice and provided refuges for some plant and animal species.

Analysis of pollen and seeds in core samples from the bottom of Yellowstone Lake reveals vegetational changes from the retreat of the Pinedale Glaciers to the present. Soon after glacial retreat, the vegetation was apparently alpine tundra or subalpine meadows with spruce, fir, and white-bark pine. The vegetation changed

rapidly to lodgepole pine forests shortly before 11,500 years ago, indicating a distinct warming trend. Lodgepole pine forest has persisted ever since.

Past and present climatic trends tell us something about the future. First, over geological time conditions and communities can change drastically. We can expect them to change in the future. Second, human impacts on climate have been so profound in recent decades that climate changes are being accelerated. The effects of climate change on communities in the Jackson Hole area could be dramatic.

SOME STUDIES OF COMMUNITY ECOLOGY IN JACKSON HOLE

Considerable research in Jackson Hole has been conducted at the community level. A brief look at some of these studies will shed light on community ecology principles and the range of research.

In one community study, coyotes on the National Elk Refuge were found to eat mostly pocket gophers, ground squirrels, buds, and carrion. Only a very small part of their diet was young elk or mule deer. Of the approximately 8,000 elk on the refuge during the winter of 1949-50, only two known cases of coyote predation occurred, both involving injured calves. Other elk were observed dying and were thought to be unable to get to their feet, but these debilitated elk were not killed by coyotes. Presumably, the abundant carrion (overall, 207 elk died from various causes) and mice diverted the coyotes' attention from these dying elk. Numbers of coyotes on the refuge were unrelated to the number of live elk.

A highly theoretical study on competition in bird communities was partially conducted in Jackson Hole. This research showed that bird species

coexisted in grasslands because of differences in habitat preferences and feeding behavior. From this study, it was learned that vegetation height could be used to predict the number of species, differences in bird feeding ecology, and bird habitat quality in grassland communities.

The waterfowl nesting sequence in spring was studied in several aquatic and willow communities in Jackson Hole. The relationship of waterfowl to various communities was investigated. The mallard, green-winged teal, and nine other species of ducks reared broods in these communities, but brood production was low probably because of a cold, wet spring and disturbance in the summer by horseback riders in the nesting area.

One of the most interesting studies in Jackson Hole attempted to determine *trophic* (food and energy) relationships and community structure of the bird fauna in six different communities—lodgepole pine, lodgepole pine-spruce-fir, spruce-fir, willow-sedge-swamp, scrub meadow, and flatland aspen. The three coniferous communities represented a successional sequence. The number of bird species using each community (bird diversity) was determined as was the number of individuals of each species and the average body weight of an individual. Bird biomass (the amount of living matter in an area at a given time) was calculated for each community. Forty-one species were classified by their community occupancy, foraging level (*figure 6.14*), and type of feeding—foliage-seed, ground-insect, timber-drilling, timber-searching, air-perching, air-soaring, foliage-insect, and foliage-nectar. Combining this information with knowledge about the energy use efficiency of birds showed that the spruce-fir community not only

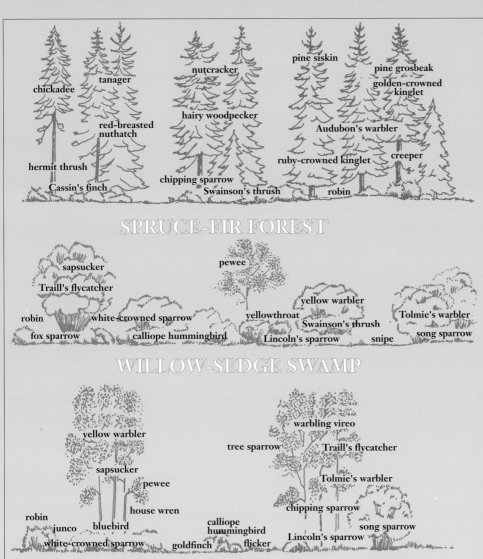

SPRUCE-FIR FOREST

WILLOW-SEDGE SWAMP

FLAT ASPEN GROVE

6.14 Bird foraging niches in three biotic communities in Jackson Hole
(after G.W. Salt, 1957, An analysis of avifaunas in the Teton Mountains of Jackson Hole, Wyoming, Condor 59:373-393)

had a greater energy flow through its vegetation and bird fauna than the lodgepole pine forest, but also that it utilized this energy more efficiently.

One study of aquatic communities in Jackson Hole examined the density, distribution, growth rate, maximum weight when mature, date of emergence, length of lifecycle, egg incubation period, drift, food habits, and parasites of the more important forms of invertebrates in the Snake River. A total of 170 species, primarily aquatic insects, was present. Drifting insects were found to be very abundant and were thought to play a major role in the ecology of the Snake River.

A study of forested glacial moraines on the valley floor resulted in quantitative descriptions of seven different communities. Lodgepole pine dominated the overstory of most communities, but subalpine fir was the dominant tree species in lower layers. Douglas fir occupied drier sites and appeared to be regenerating there. Aspen occurred on both wet and dry sites and was being replaced by conifers on many. Soil appeared to be the primary limiting factor. The moraines had more soil, less gravel and rock, and a higher water-holding capacity than soils on the generally nonforested glacial outwash.

Habitat features, food habits, and reproductive characteristics of meadow voles, mountain voles, long-tailed voles, and red-backed voles were studied to discover competitive interactions among these species. Some plant communities contained only one vole species, while others supported all four. In communities with only one or two species, competition may have kept other species out. The mountain vole occupied the widest variety of plant communities and seemed capable of existing in large numbers in all but one of them regardless of what other species were present. The mountain vole appeared to out-compete the meadow vole and restricted it from certain communities.

RECOMMENDED RESOURCES

Craighead, F. C., Jr. 1994. *For everything there is a season: The sequence of natural events in the Grand Teton-Yellowstone area.* Falcon Press, Helena, Montana. 206 pp.

Despain, D. G. 1990. *Yellowstone vegetation: Consequences of environment and history in a natural setting.* Roberts Rinehart, Boulder, Colorado. 239 pp.

Dorn, R. D. 1986. *The Wyoming landscape, 1805-1878.* Mountain West Publishing, Cheyenne, Wyoming. 94 pp.

Jeffrey, D. 1989. *Yellowstone: The great fires of 1988.* National Geographic, February:252-273.

Knight, D. H. 1994. *Mountains and plains: The ecology of Wyoming landscapes.* Yale University Press, New Haven. 338 pp.

Peters, R. L., and T. E. Lovejoy. 1992. *Global warming and biological diversity.* Yale University Press, New Haven. 386 pp.

Primm, S. A., P. Lichtman, and T. W. Clark. 1996. *Natural fire in a political environment: Lessons from Yellowstone's 1988 fires.* Northern Rockies Conservation Cooperative, Jackson, Wyoming. 38 pp.

Wuerthner, G. 1988. *Yellowstone and the fires of change.* Haggis House Publications, Inc., Salt Lake City, Utah. pp.

The Jackson Hole Ecosystem

All the many biotic communities and their abiotic environments in Jackson Hole and surrounding mountains make up the Jackson Hole ecosystem. An *ecosystem* is all the plants and animals in a given area along with their physical environment. Like all ecosystems, Jackson Hole is a self-sustaining, self-regulating assemblage of biotic and abiotic components. Ecosystems often have internal mechanisms that control the interrelations among their myriad components. There have been no comprehensive studies of the Jackson Hole ecosystem to date, although our knowledge is enhanced by the many studies done throughout the Greater Yellowstone Ecosystem, which encompasses Jackson Hole.

ECOSYSTEM BASICS

Ecosystems are made up of various components and are characterized by energy flows and material movements among these parts. *Inputs* are all the materials, energy, and organisms that enter the system, while *outputs* are things that leave the system.

Ecosystem Components—
Components are items that make up the ecosystem. Biotic components are classified by how they acquire food *(figure 7.1)*. *Producers* (or *autotrophs*) are organisms that synthesize their own food. Plants (and some algae) absorb sunlight and use its energy to make organic food from water and carbon dioxide through a process called photosynthesis. *Consumers* (or *heterotrophs*) are organisms that need organic matter (food) from their environment. These organisms must eat other organisms to survive. *Herbivores* such as elk eat plant tissue, *carnivores* such as long-tailed weasels eat animal tissue, and *omnivores* such as black bears eat both plant and animal tissue. *Decomposers* (or *saprophytes*), such as fungi and bacteria, eat dead or decaying material and transform it into inorganic material.

Abiotic components of an ecosystem include sunlight energy, physical factors such as temperature, light, and humidity, and chemical factors such as iron, sodium, potassium, proteins, fats, carbohydrates. Chemical factors include both inorganic ions and organic molecules.

Solar Energy

heat loss

Abiotic Chemicals
- Water
- Carbon Dioxide
- Oxygen
- Minerals
- Others

Decompostion

Absorption Uptake

heat loss

ABIOTIC COMPONENTS
BIOTIC COMPONENTS

Decomposers
- Bacteria
- Fungi

Death

Producers
- Green Plants
- Certain bacteria
- Algae

heat loss

Consumption

Wastes Death

Consumers
- Herbivores
- Carnivores
- Omnivores

heat loss

Teton Mountains

Gros Ventre Mountains

7.1 The Jackson Hole ecosystem is a self-sustaining system of living and non-living components driven by the sun's energy

52

Ecosystems carry out two basic processes—photosynthesis and decomposition—both of which require organisms. Organisms are made up of complex chemical compounds formed from about 40 elements, of which only six—carbon, oxygen, hydrogen, nitrogen, phosphorus, and sulfur—constitute over 95 percent of the mass of all living organisms. The fixed amount of these elements on earth must be continuously cycled through living systems from reservoirs in air, water, and soil. In *photosynthesis* plants obtain carbon, the primary element in the large organic molecules that characterize life, by using solar energy in the presence of chlorophyll to oxidize water and reduce carbon dioxide to form carbohydrates (sugars) and oxygen:

Carbon Dioxide (CO_2) + Water (H_2O) +

(Sunlight & Chlorophyll) =

Sugars (CH_2O) + Oxygen (O_2) + Heat

Plants use some of the sugars to maintain themselves, the rest are stored in different plant parts, and the oxygen is released into the air. Consumers eat plants, taking in the carbon atoms now locked by the sun's energy into the sugars. They also take in oxygen from the air and use it in respiration:

Sugars (CH_2O) + Oxygen (O_2) =

Carbon Dioxide (CO_2) + Water (H_2O) +

Heat Loss

Decomposition is "natural recycling," the process by which decomposers reduce energy-rich organic matter into carbon dioxide, water, and inorganic nutrients. Fungi, bacteria, and numerous small invertebrates are decomposers. Decomposition changes the physical and chemical structure of

Table 7.1 **Estimates of the net primary productivity of some biotic communities in Jackson Hole**

Type of Communities	Net Primary Productivity (in kilocalories/m^2/yr)
Marshes, wet meadows	900+
Lowland aspen, Kelly Warm Springs, eutrophic water	500+
Coniferous forests, deep lakes	300-900
Sagebrush	300-500
Alpine tundra, high mountain lakes	Less than 500

dead organisms into inorganic substances, which are then reused by plants in photosynthesis. This process is never ending. We know little about decomposers and the decomposition process in the Jackson Hole ecosystem.

Energy Flow—Solar radiation provides the energy essential to all life. One form of this energy is heat, which warms the earth and drives the water cycle, weather patterns, and ocean currents. Another form of energy includes the light spectrum, which photosynthetic plants use to produce carbohydrates and other organic compounds essential to nearly all life. Energy flowing from the sun to the earth is converted from physical energy to chemical energy through photosynthesis and flows on through life forms as one group of organisms consumes others.

The amount of energy accumulated by an organism is *production*. The rate at which green plants convert solar energy to chemical energy through photosynthesis is known as *gross primary productivity*. Plants use some of this energy for growth and maintenance.

The rest, which is stored in plants and is thus available to animals, is *net primary productivity*, which is measured in calories (or kilocalories) of plant material per square meter (or square kilometer) per time period (hour, day, month, or year). The meadow community, like that on the National Elk Refuge, has one of the highest primary productivities, whereas deep, cold mountain lakes and alpine tundra have the lowest *(table 7.1). Secondary productivity* is the accumulation of energy by consumers, that is, animals and decomposers. A grasshopper assimilates about 30 percent of the grass it consumes, and a deer mouse assimilates 85 percent or more of what it eats. Consumers use the energy for body maintenance, respiration, growth, and reproduction to the extent they can. Energy left over from these essential activities is converted to fat and stored in the body.

Biomass is the total weight of living tissue in organisms. There is more biomass of green plants in an ecosystem than there is of elk, which consume the vegetation, and even less biomass in carnivores and scavengers that eat the

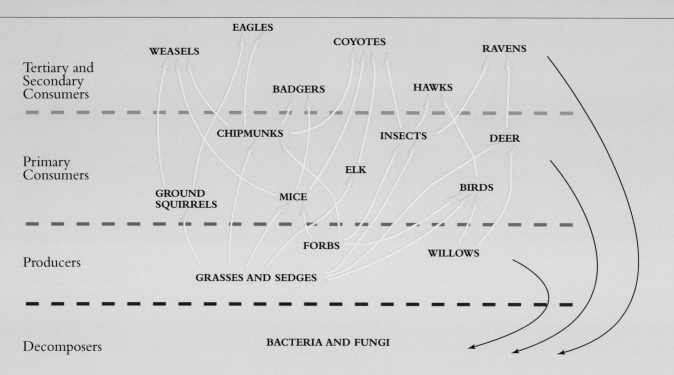

Tertiary and
Secondary
Consumers

Primary
Consumers

Producers

Decomposers

7.2 A partial and simplified food web on the National Elk Refuge

elk. The amount of energy stored in biomass is the *standing crop*. The standing crop of vegetation is greater than that of elk or wolves. In Jackson Hole the biomass accumulated in new plant growth and new animals born each year is recycled seasonally as plants and animals die and decompose.

The energy in plants is consumed by animals and passed along as one organism eats another in a series of steps, or *trophic* (food) *levels*, called a *food chain*. In most ecosystems, food chains have many cross links, that is, any one organism usually consumes many different kinds of foods. These food chains are called *food webs (figure 7.2)*.

An important characteristic of food chains and webs is that energy transfer from one trophic level to another is never 100 percent efficient. The *Second Law of Thermodynamics* states that some energy is lost in all energy transfers, mostly as heat. All energy is ultimately transferred as heat to the environment and lost from life forms. Commonly, only 5 to 15 percent of the energy in one trophic level is transferred to the

next, while 85 to 95 percent is used to maintain life processes or is lost as heat. Because of the energy loss at each link in the chain, the length of food chains is limited. Nearly all food chains have three or four trophic levels. This decline in the available energy and the number of organisms in successively higher trophic levels can be illustrated in *pyramids of energy and numbers (figure 7.3)*.

Food webs illustrate that all life depends on energy from the sun which green plants make available to other organisms by converting it to chemical energy through photosynthesis. The shorter the food chain, the more efficient it is. Measurement of energy flow and efficiencies is one of the important tasks of ecosystem ecologists.

Material Movements—All ecosystems are maintained by two interconnected processes — the transfer of energy and the cycling of materials or nutrients. The flow of energy is essential for nutrient cycling. More technically, *biogeochemical cycling* (bio = life, geo = earth, chemical = atoms and molecules) is the continuous circulation

of chemicals through organisms, soil, water, and air. Solar energy drives biogeochemical cycles. While most chemicals are cycled, energy is not. Energy flows in one direction through ecosystems and is ultimately dissipated as heat into the environment.

Biogeochemical cycles involve both biotic and abiotic components *(figure 7.4)*. Plants and animals produce complex molecules from atoms through physiological processes. The atoms and molecules are passed from one organism to another in food chains. When organisms die, they are decomposed and atoms are released back into the nutrient pool in the soil, air, and water so that plants and other autotrophs can reuse them to make new organic matter. The atoms in your body have been recycled many times in the many millions of years they have existed.

Biogeochemical cycles are made up of two large compartments or sites where materials are located. The larger *reservoir compartment* is abiotic and mostly unavailable to living organisms.

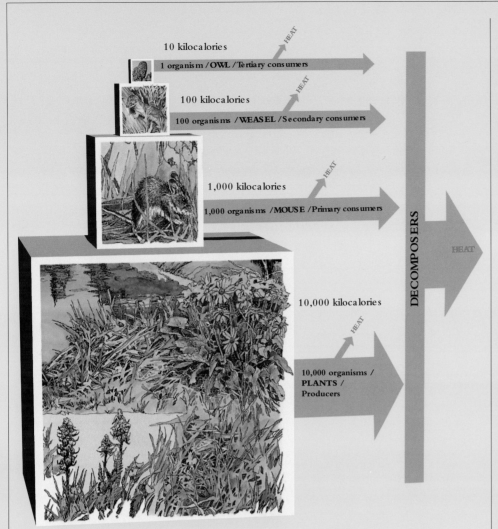

10 kilocalories

1 organism /OWL /Tertiary consumers

HEAT

100 kilocalories

100 organisms /WEASEL /Secondary consumers

HEAT

1,000 kilocalories

1,000 organisms /MOUSE /Primary consumers

HEAT

DECOMPOSERS

HEAT

10,000 kilocalories

10,000 organisms / PLANTS / Producers

HEAT

7.3 Pyramids of energy and numbers of organisms in a hypothetical ecosystem

The much smaller *cycling compartment* is more active and is available to organisms. Materials are exchanged fairly rapidly over time between organisms and their surrounding environment in a unending process.

Biogeochemical cycles also take place in two forms—gaseous and sedimentary. *Gaseous cycles*, global in scale, have as their major reservoir the atmosphere. Four major gaseous cycles are vital to life— oxygen, carbon, nitrogen, and water vapor. In the global *oxygen cycle* this element moves between the atmosphere, oceans, sediments, and living organisms. The *carbon cycle* moves carbon, which is the basic component of organic compounds and organisms and the major

element fixed by plants in photosynthesis. The *nitrogen cycle* moves nitrogen and nitrogen-containing chemicals through the ecosphere. The process of converting atmospheric nitrogen to ammonia or nitrate is *nitrogen fixation*; some plants are very efficient at this process. Finally, the *water cycle* moves water between the oceans, the atmosphere, and land systems.

The *sedimentary cycles* circulate the mineral elements in the earth's crust that are required by organisms. These essential elements are obtained from inorganic sources, such as minerals dissolved in water in the soil or in streams and lakes. Rock and minerals are the main reservoirs. Some mineral

salts are released through weathering. Plants in turn assimilate these minerals, which are then passed along through food chains. The key sedimentary cycles are sulfur and phosphorus. The *sulfur cycle* has both gaseous and sedimentary parts. Bacteria are vital to this cycle. The *phosphorus cycle* is entirely sedimentary since no phosphorous exists in the atmosphere. Phosphorus is in short supply almost everywhere.

All ecosystems tend to maintain a dynamic steady state, commonly called "balance of nature," where the input and output of energy and matter in an ecosystem are kept in equilibrium by a system of positive and negative feedbacks that operate like the thermostat for a furnace. A simple example of a natural feedback system is the vole-weasel population cycle mentioned in chapter 5 *(figure 7.5)*. There are vast numbers of feedback systems in ecosystems that influence rates of biogeochemical cycling and energy flow.

BIOLOGICAL DIVERSITY
Biological diversity, or *biodiversity* for short, is simply the diversity of life, which varies from one ecosystem to another. Most people tend to think in terms of individual organisms or species or sometimes populations. Rarely do they think in terms of biodiversity—all the many plants and animals in a region. Ecologists studying patterns and processes of life are interested in three levels of biodiversity—genetic, species, and community diversity—and in the status of each. Species diversity is best known in Jackson Hole. The forests have fewer than a dozen tree species, compared to forests in the Great Smoky Mountains, which are far richer with 125 species. We have less knowledge about community diversity in Jackson Hole and far less about genetic diversity.

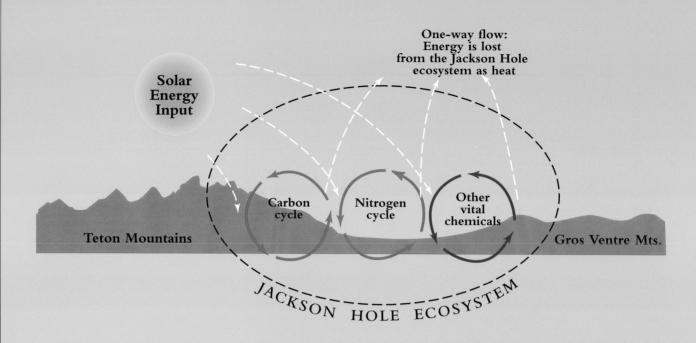

One-way flow:
Energy is lost
from the Jackson Hole
ecosystem as heat

Solar
Energy
Input

Carbon cycle

Nitrogen cycle

Other vital chemicals

Teton Mountains

Gros Ventre Mts.

JACKSON HOLE ECOSYSTEM

7.4 Energy flow and biogeochemical cycles in Jackson Hole

Species diversity is a measure of how many different plant and animal species are present in a community or ecosystem and their relative abundance. The total number of species in an ecosystem is *species richness*. Other aspects of species diversity are measured, too, such as *spread*, or the spatial configuration of species over landscapes as well as diversity within and between communities and ecosystems.

Ecologists have some knowledge of species diversity in the Jackson Hole ecosystem, which is part of the larger Greater Yellowstone Ecosystem. Knowledge of the microflora and microfauna in Greater Yellowstone is limited, but it is estimated that there are probably a few thousand species. There are about 1,700 species of vascular plants, about 7 percent of which are threatened. Invertebrates probably number in the tens of thousands, but except for a few species, their status is unknown. Among vertebrates there are 12 fish, 12 amphibians and reptiles, about 300 birds, and 60 mammals. About 3 to 12 percent of each

of these classes are threatened depending on the group.

This species diversity is not uniformly spread across all the biotic communities. Some communities are much richer in species than others. In Jackson Hole, species diversity is highest in structurally diverse terrestrial communities, such as mixed willow and aspen. Jackson Hole and the Greater Yellowstone Ecosystem have about the same number of species as areas of comparable size in Siberia, for example, with the same kinds of biotic communities. Large tracts of relatively undisturbed, temperate, forested areas at the same latitude and elevation worldwide are more or less similar in species diversity.

The major question, though, is what sets the limits to diversity in any given ecosystem. Some simple observations have been made. First, there is a gradual increase in species diversity from the arctic to the equator. Second, species diversity tends to increase with advancing ecological succession. Third,

larger communities tend to have more species. Fourth, diversity is greatest in climax communities and even there it tends to increase over time. These observations have led to a number of theories to account for differences in diversity.

There are four major theories about the patterns we see in biodiversity. First is the *time hypothesis*, which says that greater diversity is found in older communities. This suggests that the alpine tundra is younger than the lowland willow and aspen communities. It also implies that it takes time for species to disperse into unoccupied habitats. Since parts of Jackson Hole were scoured down to bedrock by glaciers about 10,000 years ago, some species that could live here have not had time to move into the area. Second is the *spatial complexity hypothesis*, which explains diversity in terms of environmental complexity. The more complex and diverse an environment, the more niches available to plants and animals. In lakes, for example, diversity increases from deep open waters to the shore line, that is, as the structural complexity increases, submerged and emergent vegetation also increases. Third is the *productivity hypothesis*, which says that diversity may be a function of environmental productivity. If primary productivity is high, then species diversity will be high. There are examples, however, from other ecosystems where high productivity does not necessarily lead to high species diversity. Fourth is the *Slobodkin and Sanders theory*, which says that diversity is highest where biotic interactions promote diversity. In the alpine tundra, for example, the environment is dramatically controlled by abiotic physical and chemical features that significantly determine the structure of the community and thus limit its species diversity. In willow and aspen communities, on the other hand, plants and animals are important in the community's structure, and thus biotic interactions are greater and diversity is higher. In actuality, these four theories

are compatible, and in all likelihood, species diversity is a function of a complex mix of all four.

Genetic diversity is a lower and less obvious level of diversity within species. If we examine two individual coyotes, we would find that they differ in certain ways, some of which would be the result of genetic differences. *Genes* are the units of heredity. They are like words in the library of life, and we are just now learning to read them. Genes are naturally selected over time by the environment, that is, genes that fail to help a species adapt to its environment are weeded out while those that do are rewarded by increased reproduction. The pattern of genetic change caused in a population by this process is *evolution*. Individual vertebrates are made up of thousands of genes. A mouse or a human each has about 100,000 genes. Usually, the greater the species diversity, the greater the genetic diversity, although there are some exceptions. A few species—cheetahs are a well known

example—show almost no genetic diversity among individuals.

Genetic diversity is a direct measure of the basic diversity in living forms. One famous instance of unique genetic diversity is *Thermus aquaticus*, a bacterium living in the hot springs of Yellowstone that is found nowhere else on earth. One of its genes was featured on the cover of *Science* magazine in 1989 as "the molecule of the year." This gene, which can function in water at 160° F, produces enzymes that can copy genetic material in other species. Already it has revolutionized certain aspects of medicine and criminology, and the minimum value today of its commercial applications is $300 million and growing.

There are no measures of the actual genetic diversity in the Jackson Hole or Greater Yellowstone ecosystems. If there were, it would show that there are billions of different kinds of genes in existence currently. These genes are active minute by minute in

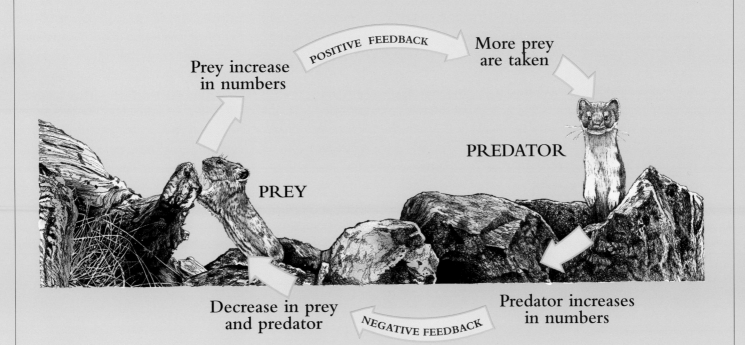

7.5 A simplified feedback system between prey and predator in Jackson Hole

organisms as they carry out essential life processes (such as cellular physiology, reproduction). In turn they are acted upon by natural selection in an endless process of adaptation, reproduction, and survival. A physical manifestation of the genetic diversity in the region is the many different kinds of plant and animal species that live here.

Community diversity (sometimes called *ecosystem* or *landscape diversity*) is at the big end of biodiversity. The Jackson Hole ecosystem is made up of about eleven biotic communities, each with a relatively unique assemblage of plants and animals and genes. Biological diversity is especially high in *ecotones* (the edges where two communities meet) because they include a mix of plants and animals from each adjacent community. The sizes of the communities and their compositions may change over time. Natural disturbances such as fires, landslides, and floods are essential to maintain some communities. Different ecosystems have different community diversity; obviously, the biotic community diversity of Alaska is different from that of Florida. Healthy landscapes usually require a mix of communities.

Sometimes communities appear as natural islands of habitat. Blacktail Butte, a four-square-mile hill just east of Moose in the center of Jackson Hole, is a good example. The forests on the butte are surrounded by an "ocean" of dry sagebrush that isolates some of the butte's species from other forested habitats. The butte also has a spring-fed stream, but this water habitat is separated by nearly a mile from the nearest other running water. Roads and human activities serve further to isolate the butte. Ecologists use *island biogeographic theory* to study naturally occurring "ecological islands" and the biodiversity

they contain.

The number of species on an undisturbed island (or in any undisturbed ecosystem) tends to reach an *equilibrium*—that is, some species may go extinct but others will immigrate and establish new populations so that the overall number of species on the island stays more or less constant. A mathematical relationship known as the *species-area relationship* has been discerned between the area of an island and the number of species living on that island.

If Blacktail Butte were part of an undisturbed larger ecosystem, we would expect to find about 23 mammal species (excluding bats) there. But if the butte were totally isolated, we would expect only two mammal species to live there. About 21 mammal species would go extinct as a result of isolation. Currently, about nine mammal species are known to occupy the butte. The biological diversity on the butte could be further isolated from that on both sides of the valley by the continuing effects of removing irrigation water from Ditch Creek, a naturally occurring dispersal corridor connecting the butte to forests on the eastern side of the valley. Additional, wider, and more heavily traveled roads encircling the butte and bigger bridges could have the same isolating effect. These and other factors could cause extinctions in Grand Teton National Park.

This simple account shows what can result from the isolation of ecological islands. The Jackson Hole ecosystem and the Greater Yellowstone Ecosystem, as well as many national parks in the United States and elsewhere, are increasingly cut off from surrounding lands with abundant biodiversity. As these "protected" lands become more and more isolated, extinction rates can be expected to

increase. Even the 2.2-million-acre Yellowstone National Park is highly vulnerable to this problem.

Today humans affect biodiversity in many ways that are harmful. Our activities often fragment habitats, reduce and isolate populations, and simplify biotic communities and ecosystems with the result that we cause and accelerate the extinction process. Perhaps as much as 20 percent of the earth's biological diversity is currently threatened with extinction because of human activities. The proportion of biodiversity that is endangered is expected to rise unless appropriate actions are taken soon.

Biodiversity at all three levels— genetic, species, and community—is critical to the functioning of nature and to the sustenance of the human enterprise. In a recent poll, scientists identified the loss of biodiversity (declining plant and animal populations, or the extinction problem) as one of the top four problems confronting humanity today, along with human population growth, pollution, and global climate change. The Canadian journal *Global Biodiversity* estimated that humans currently use about 55 percent of all solar energy striking all land on earth—leaving only 45 percent for all plants and animals. If the human population doubles in the next few decades, as it is expected to do, then biodiversity everywhere will be severely threatened. Unfortunately, the loss of biodiversity is an issue that is virtually invisible to many people compared to other environmental problems. As a result, its importance is grossly underappreciated, and little attention is being given to remedies. Ensuring a sustainable future not only for Jackson Hole's biodiversity but also for the diversity of life around the world should be of the highest priority.

RESTORATION ECOLOGY

One goal of modern ecology is to protect biological diversity and ecosystems. This can be achieved by conserving the diversity that already exists in wilderness and other natural areas and by restoring species to areas where they have been extirpated, even in areas that support many people. Restoration ecology is a branch of ecology that tackles the job of ecological healing or rehabilitation.

There are many species in Jackson Hole and environs that need better protection to restore or keep the ecosystem intact. Some rare species, such as the peregrine falcon, are undergoing considerable restoration attention. For such populations to recover and resume their former ecological roles in these ecosystem, their populations and ranges will have to grow. Even if their populations do expand, they will need continuing management and protection. But restoring threatened and endangered species to ecologically significant levels can be difficult. Ecological restoration efforts for the grizzly bear and wolf are two illustrations of the complexity of this process.

Grizzly Bear Restoration— Grizzly bears are larger and more heavily built than most other bears (*figure 7.6*). They attain a weight of 400 to more than 1,000 pounds and a length of more than six feet. The color of their fur may be black, gray, brown, tan, yellow, cream, or red. The light-colored guard hairs give this bear its grizzled appearance.

The grizzly bear's ecological role is omnivory with an extremely broad diet. Grizzlies prey on elk calves, ground squirrels, and spawning fish, consume large quantities of green plants, roots, and berries, and also scavenge winter- and road-killed animals. Bears are part

7.6 Grizzly bear

of complex and diverse trophic relationships, which affect the structure, energy flow, and biogeochemical cycles of the ecosystem. The magnitude of these effects are under study.

Grizzlies are primarily solitary animals that live as individuals or family groups. They breed in June or July and give birth while in hibernation in February. Young stay with the mother for up to three years and become sexually mature at about 4.5 years. Grizzly bears range throughout the Greater Yellowstone Ecosystem today and occupy about 6 million acres. They require spacious habitat; individual home ranges vary from 50 to 800+ square miles. These ecological and behavioral features can bring the grizzly bear into direct conflict with humans and also make it vulnerable to local extinction. In turn, this makes the restoration task difficult.

The history of grizzly bears' relationship to humans, their destruction, and conservation makes a fascinating story. Grizzly bears formerly ranged over most of western North America and were once common in Jackson Hole. Around 1900 some people realized that the grizzly's numbers were declining so rapidly in the Rocky Mountains that it could be saved only in Yellowstone National Park, if at all. Today Yellowstone and grizzly bears are almost synonymous in the minds of many people around the world.

Knowing about the grizzly's basic biology and ecology is an essential first step in restoring the species. Yellowstone's remnant population, which was listed under the 1973 Endangered Species Act as threatened, has been the focus of various recovery plans, millions of dollars, and concerted conservation effort since 1975. Restoring this population has been a challenge because of the bear's large size and space requirements and complex ecological needs, but also because of the finite size and ecological variability of available habitats within the ecosystem and the increasing human use of the region. Fundamentally, humans have not been willing to give bears the minimum space necessary for a viable population to persist.

Disagreement continues about how well the grizzly population is being restored in the Greater Yellowstone Ecosystem, and the case is being debated vigorously in scientific, legal, and public arenas. Some people claim that the bear is recovered or nearly so and that, as a result, restoration efforts and conservation can be relaxed and turned over by the federal government to the states for routine management. Other people say that data are inadequate to determine the bear's current status or the success of restoration efforts and that continued effort is needed to ensure its future.

A few hundred grizzly bears still reside in Greater Yellowstone, management has improved, and the public is better educated about this animal. Problems remain, however. In recent years, the population has expanded south into the Jackson Hole area. As a result, bears have come into contact with cattle on grazing allotments in Bridger-Teton National Forest and Grand Teton National Park. A few cattle have been killed—inflaming historic controversies over bear conservation and the legitimacy of certain human uses of public lands. Bear "proponents" want cattle

removed from the national park and forest grazing allotments and moved south outside bear range. Bear "opponents" want bears moved or killed and cattle production protected by government actions and subsidies. Practical solutions still need to be worked out. Grizzly restoration is truly a test of the understanding and commitment of humans to restoring and maintaining structurally and functionally healthy ecosystems.

Wolf Restoration—Wolves formerly occurred throughout most of North America. The species was native to the Jackson Hole and Greater Yellowstone ecosystems, but by the 1940s the population was functionally extinct. The last Yellowstone wolf was killed in 1926. Wolves are the only species that was totally extirpated in the Greater Yellowstone region. The absence of wolves, which function as top-level carnivores that influence prey numbers and distributions over large areas (especially in winter), has no doubt had significant effects on the ecology of many animals and plants in the ecosystem.

Wolf restoration has been an extremely complex and controversial challenge with sociopolitical and biological dimensions. The main obstacle is the heavy burden of negative symbolism that the wolf carries, the legacy of our European forebears. Colonists came to this continent already imbued with a hatred and fear

of wolves that led to centuries of massive extermination programs. As with grizzlies, the restoration of wolves will require changes in human behavior and management practices more than anything else.

The largest wild member of the canid family, the gray wolf reaches 90-100 pounds and 5-6.5 feet nose to tail (*figure 7.7*). It varies in color from coal black to gray to creamy white. The wolf's ecological role is as the preeminent predator of large ungulates, including elk, deer, and moose, although they also eat small animals such as beaver, squirrels, and other small rodents. A wolf consumes 8-12 pounds of meat per day, or the equivalent of about eight elk per year. Wolves may eat livestock, but most wolves living near livestock do not prey on domestic animals. In Minnesota and western Canada, for instance, wolves on average kill about one stock animal out of every 1,000 grazed each year. The basic social unit, the pack, consists of two to 16 wolves. Packs use territories of 50 to 300 square miles, boundaries of which are delineated by howling and scent marking. Breeding occurs in February and, following a 63-day gestation, four to seven pups are born. Pups grow rapidly and by early fall are ready to travel with older animals. Wolves generally become sexually mature at two years.

Formal efforts to restore wolves to this region began in the early 1970s. In 1973 when the Endangered Species Act was passed, the northern Rocky Mountain wolf (a subspecies) was listed as endangered, a designation that required the federal government to take action to restore the species. A recovery team was appointed in 1974, and the recovery plan was approved in 1980. The 1987 revised plan called for translocating wolves to Yellowstone

7.7 The gray wolf

National Park, although the restoration area was eventually expected to extend south to the National Elk Refuge. The plan called for establishing 100 wolves in 10 packs inside the restoration zone.

In 1988 Congress funded a study of what might happen if wolves were reintroduced to Yellowstone and how wolves might affect the ecology of other animal populations in the region. In 1990 a bill was introduced in Congress to restore wolves to Yellowstone. A draft environmental impact statement (EIS) was prepared in 1993, and over 160,000 public comments came in, nearly all in support of wolf restoration. The final EIS was released in May 1994, and various official decisions, rules, and court cases opposing the reintroduction were settled that year. Thus, after a long, complex planning and public participation process, the stage was set to return wolves to this region.

On January 12, 1995, eight captured Canadian wolves arrived in Yellowstone National Park, and six more wolves were delivered on January 19. The pens holding the wolves were opened in March and wolves moved out to roam freely in the ecosystem. In 1996, 17 more wolves were brought in, held in large pens, and later released to join the other free-ranging wolves. There are no plans to bring in more wolves.

The restoration program to date has been very successful. The translocated wolves are displaying ecological patterns as expected, according to ongoing study. To date, they have mostly stayed within or near Yellowstone National Park, although a few individuals are traveling widely. It is expected that they will eventually settle into stable packs and territories. The recovery target of 100 wolves could be reached within a few years. Wolves first moved onto the National Elk Refuge in

7.8 A ranger in Grand Teton National Park tells visitors about the history of Menor's Ferry

the winter of 1998-99. There will probably always be some opposition to wolves, and careful management of both wolf and human activities will need to be part of the continuing restoration effort.

This restoration ecology effort is one of the highest profile programs ever undertaken. With the eventual restoration of wolves, grizzly bears, and other threatened or endangered species, the Jackson Hole ecosystem and the Greater Yellowstone Ecosystem will once again be complete in terms of ecological components and processes.

GRAND TETON NATIONAL PARK

Grand Teton National Park makes up a significant part of the Jackson Hole ecosystem (figure 7.8). The primary purpose of the National Park Service in administering natural areas is to maintain a park's ecosystem in as pristine a condition as possible. Ecological processes, including plant succession and the natural regulation of animal numbers, are permitted to proceed as

they did before the presence of white settlers who colonized the region, and human uses of parks must be generally nonconsumptive. Thus the National Park Service is in the ecological restoration business and committed to maintaining intact, fully functional ecosystems for the benefit and enjoyment of people.

This deceptively simple mission is difficult to implement in practice. Modern parks were established with artificial boundaries often unrelated to ecological boundaries. Modern park management practices include removing introduced exotic species, restoring natural processes like predation and fire, regulating potentially harmful tourist uses, and educating the public about these and other ecological requirements. Despite extensive human impacts on the parks, though, most park biotic communities are comparatively intact or have some reasonable potential for being returned to a pristine state. Much of the research in national parks today focuses on documenting pristine ecological conditions and

The Tetons viewed from the shore of Jackson Lake in the northern part of Grand Teton National Park

processes, determining the completeness of park ecosystems, and developing management techniques to maintain or restore pristine conditions.

Several ecological management techniques are applicable to Grand Teton National Park. For example, natural fire, which was common in Jackson Hole until about 1900, is being restored to the extent possible. The park gained national news coverage in 1974 when the highly visible, lightning-caused Waterfall Canyon fire, which covered about 3,500 acres, was allowed to burn for over three months until it was naturally extinguished by snow. The extensive 1988 fires again put Grand Teton and Yellowstone National Parks under national scrutiny. Periodic population irruptions of native insects such as the mountain pine beetle, which were once thought to be harmful, are better understood today simply as typical ecosystem processes. These insect-forest interactions have occurred naturally for millennia, and so attempts to control

these insects have been discontinued.

Grand Teton National Park does not include all the ecological requirements of elk, most of which must winter outside the park on the National Elk Refuge. The elk population is managed by public hunting in parts of the park as well as outside, and it is supplementally fed during winter on the refuge. Since the elk are subjected to different management policies by different state and federal agencies in different parts of the valley at different times of year, management of the park's elk as a component of an undisturbed ecosystem is not possible.

Perhaps the most important function of Grand Teton National Park is to explain the ecosystem concept and its processes to the park's visitors. A high quality environment has not yet become a national priority, despite current interest in environmental problems such as pollution. Understanding of the park ecosystem can help visitors appreciate problems such as environmental degra-

dation, plant and animal extinctions, and human overpopulation. The contrast between the relatively pristine conditions of Grand Teton National Park and many degraded landscapes and urban areas profoundly affects many park visitors. As a relatively complete and natural ecosystem, Grand Teton National Park can help promote an environmental ethic that extends well beyond the park's boundaries.

RECOMMENDED RESOURCES

Brunner, R. D., and T. W. Clark. 1997. *A practice-based approach to ecosystem management.* Conservation Biology 11:48-58.

Casey, D., and T. W. Clark. 1996. *Tales of the wolf: Fifty-one stories of wolf encounters in the wild.* Homestead Press, Moose, Wyoming. 294 pp.

Clark, T. W., and S. C. Minta. 1994. *Greater Yellowstone's future: Prospects for ecosystem science, management, and policy.* Homestead Press, Moose, Wyoming. 160 pp.

Cook, R. S., ed. 1993. *Ecological issues on reintroducing wolves into Yellowstone National Park,* Scientific Monograph NPLS/NRYELL/NRSM-93/22:1-328.

Fritts, S. H., E. E. Bangs, J. A. Fontaine, W. G. Brewster, and J. F. Gore. 1995. *Restoring wolves to the northern Rocky Mountains of the United States.* Pp. 107-126 in L. N. Carbyn, S. H. Fritts, and D. R. Seip, eds., Ecology and conservation of wolves in a changing world. Canadian Circumpolar Institute, University of Alberta, Edmonton.

Golley, R. B. 1993. *A history of the ecosystem concept in ecology: More than the sum of the parts.* Yale University Press, New Haven, Connecticut. 254 pp.

Mattson, D. J., S. Herrero, R. G. Wright, and C. M. Pease. 1996. *Science and management of Rocky Mountain grizzly bears.* Conservation Biology 10:1,013-1,012.

Meffe, G. K., and C. R. Carroll. 1994. *Principles of conservation biology.* Sinauer Associates, Inc., Sunderland, Massachusetts. 600 pp.

Ecology of Humans

Like all other life forms, humans have an ecology in Jackson Hole, too. Today, in fact, we are a major component of the ecosystem. As living organisms, we have limits of tolerance although we can attenuate these limits by building warm, dry homes and dressing and behaving appropriately. As a population, our numbers, dispersion, density, birth and death rates, immigration and emigration rates, and age and sex structure change over time. As members of biotic communities, we interact with many species through fishing and hunting, agriculture, modification of vegetation, and displacement (using other species' habitats for recreation, building, and commercial activities). As ecosystem components, we participate in energy flows and biogeochemical cycles, and we are limited by the second law of thermodynamics. Too little energy and too few materials exist in the Jackson Hole ecosystem to support the current human population year round. Energy must be imported via electric lines, oil and gas, and firewood. Materials must be brought in to support us, including human and animal food, building materials, and manufactured goods. In addition, many of our material wastes are exported to Sublette County and buried in landfills.

HISTORICAL TRENDS IN HUMAN USE OF JACKSON HOLE

Human history in Jackson Hole goes back a long time, but within the last 150 years our ecological role and manipulations have reached levels that have significantly altered the original Jackson Hole ecosystem. The history of the American West is a complex and fascinating one, and Jackson Hole illustrates periods of exploration, settlement, and modernization.

Early Occupation—Humans were present as long as 11,000 years ago when glaciers still covered parts of Jackson Hole. Early humans apparently did not winter in the valley. Evidence of people in southern Jackson Hole dates back only 5,000 years when a large lake in the Gros Ventre River drainage (similar to Lower Slide Lake) suddenly broke through a natural dam. Water probably 300 feet deep flooded the southern half of Jackson Hole and obliterated all earlier evidence of human presence.

Early humans reached Jackson Hole through the Yellowstone region to the north, over Teton Pass to the west, via Bacon Ridge in the Gros Ventre Mountains and following the Gros Ventre River from the east, or possibly along the Hoback River in the south. These travel routes were used seasonally. Apparently early humans stayed mostly east of the Snake River, possibly because the river had only two good

Canoers enjoy Jackson Lake

8.1 A Native American family in Jackson Hole

8.2 Fur trappers helped eliminate many of Jackson Hole's large predators

fords, one at the north end of Jackson Lake and the other far to the south at the mouth of the Hoback River. Crossing to the west side may not have been worth the risk involved since everything required for survival, such as large animals, food plants, and material for tools and weapons, was more abundant and easily obtained east of the river.

The journals of early white explorers and trappers indicate that two Native American cultures existed from 1811 to the 1860s (figure 8.1). The Bannock, Snake (later called Wind River Shoshoni), Gros Ventre, Crow, Blackfeet, and Flathead tribes used horses. They passed through Jackson Hole from time to time on their way to fur trade rendezvous or on raiding parties, but none claimed the valley. The other culture consisted of nomadic pedestrian tribes, principally the Sheepeaters. They were a shy, wary people, never numerous, who used dogs for hunting and carrying supplies. They ate plants during summer and bighorn sheep during winter. Their small, widely-spaced bands were primarily family groups that seldom contained more than four adult males. A group met by white travelers in the 1830s in Hayden Valley in Yellowstone consisted of six men, seven women, eight to 10 children, and 30 dogs.

With the coming of fur trappers in the early 1800s, Indian numbers and range were diminished by introduced diseases, destruction of important food resources such as bison, usurpation of other resources (such as land and timber), and by direct killing. The trappers took beaver, muskrats, American martens, and other furbearers. The number of white trappers, the period they resided in the valley, their uses of the ecosystem, and the effects of their presence are unknown. Little is known,

8.4 An early view of the town of Jackson

8.3 The National Elk Refuge was established in 1912

too, about human use of the Jackson Hole region between the end of the fur trade in the mid-1830s, and about 1860, which began a period of exploration that lasted until the first settlers came to Jackson Hole in 1884.

Settlement, Political Divisions, and Resource Use—When Wyoming became a state in 1890, at least 64 people lived in Jackson Hole making their living through subsistence agriculture, hunting, and some guiding. Over the next decade the isolated valley became known as an outlaw hideout. The late 1800s and early 1900s saw the near extermination of several large predator species, reduction of other wildlife populations, and increasing human influence on natural biotic communities (*figure 8.2*).

In 1872 Yellowstone National Park was established, and in 1897 the Teton Forest Reservation, which included the Teton Mountain Range, was set up. The National Elk Refuge was established in 1912 and subsequently enlarged (*figure 8.3*). In 1929 the most scenic part of the

Teton Range was set aside as Grand Teton National Park. Much of the adjacent valley floor was included in the Jackson Hole National Monument in 1943. In 1950 the original national park and the monument were combined into the present Grand Teton National Park.

During this period the regional landscape was subdivided into federal jurisdictions, states, counties, and towns (*figure 8.4*). This parceling out of the ecosystem brought the region into the mainstream economic system. Relatively stable relationships among

8.5 *Fish this large were abundant in the valley sixty years ago but are much more rare today.*

county, state, and federal governments as well as direct connections to markets paved the way to exploit natural resources in systematic and relatively large-scale ways. These relationships and practices continued unchallenged. Jackson Hole's resources came to be used more and more. Animals were trapped for furs and hunted for meat, forests were cut, minerals were mined, rangeland was grazed, crops were grown, and tourists were entertained on the mountain trails and the rivers *(figure 8-5)*.

By the late 1970s many residents felt that resource use by tourists and residents, including hunting, fishing, floating the river, backcountry hiking, and camping, was approaching saturation levels. Attention was given to the regulation of hunting and fishing to ensure that these resources would not be overused. Studies were done to analyze levels of river traffic, snowmobile and backcountry use. Facilities in

Jackson Hole became increasingly overwhelmed during peak tourist visitation. Talk of "downtown" problems such as traffic congestion, lack of parking, and crime surfaced each year from June to September, the main tourist season. Reasonably priced housing was in shorter supply. Wages remained low, yet Jackson consistently had the highest cost of living in the state. It is more difficult, however, to define desired upper limits of human population density and tourist traffic than it is to set limits on hunting, fishing, or timber harvests.

Finding Balance—The net effect of human colonization is clear—the quality of Jackson Hole's natural ecosystem clearly has diminished over the last 150 years. Many species of plants and wildlife have been affected, some nearly obliterated, and some others have been seriously reduced in numbers. Seasonal patterns for many animals have been drastically changed.

Water quality has been reduced. And human crowding exists, certainly during the summer. Developments on private lands throughout Jackson Hole are growing rapidly. Some people view these changes as progress, others view them as unacceptable degradation. After several iterations of town and county planning in recent decades, these many concerns have not yet been laid to rest. Hard questions plague residents and leaders about the nature of the ecosystem and the character of its human community. What constitutes an overload on ecological systems in Jackson Hole? What ought to be humans' ecological role in Jackson Hole? How can human use of the Jackson Hole ecosystem be made sustainable over the long term? How do we resolve these and related issues democratically?

As people move to Jackson Hole or visit here, they become part of the "Boone paradox." Seeking a quiet life, Daniel Boone left the pressures of the settlements and moved to the frontier. In so doing, he paved the way for many more new settlers and increased pressures of the kind he was trying to escape. In short, he helped to destroy what he most valued. Millions of people visit Jackson Hole annually so this cannot legitimately be considered an isolated, frontier-like, mountain valley. Yet the valley's economic life depends upon maintaining a high quality environment that will continue to attract tourists. Finding a balance is not easy.

HUMAN ECOLOGY

Although the accomplishments of human culture are enormous, humanity is ultimately governed—even today—by the fundamental ecological principles that hold true for all organisms. These basic environmental relationships are often overlooked in discussions about our community and its future. It may be easier to comprehend how ecological and evolutionary forces affected early humans than how they affect us here and now. So let's look at human ecology going far back in time.

Human Ecology through History—Early hunter-gatherers had few, if any, ecological characteristics not also found in animals. Our status in biotic communities was not very different from that of other animal members. Our population size was probably in dynamic equilibrium with ecological forces. We depended on the energy flowing through the ecosystem and the cycling of materials. We used plants and other animals for shelter, protection against enemies, food, and medicine—just as we do today. Our niche in the community was comparable to that of the large carnivores and omnivores, and we had to compete with them for the essentials of life.

When humans became agriculturists and finally technologists, we changed from ordinary members of the ecosystem to a dominant ecological force. Since 1900 humans have clearly been dominant in Jackson Hole. In the process of technologically modifying our environment to suit ourselves, we determined to a large extent what other species would be permitted to associate with us. We are not unique in assuming an ecological dominance on earth. Dinosaurs were dominant for 100 million years compared to humanity's few thousand. We have not yet achieved complete dominance in the polar regions, deserts, tropical rain forests, or oceans. Even in temperate areas, catastrophes such as dust bowls, desertification, extinctions, pollution, and other undesirable events can occur despite our efforts to control nature.

Today we are still as dependent on plants for nutrition, energy, and materials as were early humans. But we have created many simplified ecosystems in which our needs can be fulfilled more efficiently because we have replaced energy from humans and draft animals with energy from fossil fuels. We have also increased our dominance by reducing population-limiting factors such as mortality from predation and disease and by increasing food production through agriculture. As a result, the human population and its rate of growth has increased greatly since the beginning of the Industrial Revolution about 1760 in Britain (*table 8.1*).

Many ecologists and anthropologists believe that the gravest question facing humanity in the twenty-first century is whether we can regulate our population. Our population must stabilize at a level best suited to the long-term productivity of natural and human-dominated ecosystems. Our relatively comfortable physical existence and our many rich cultures depend on it. The more we know about the "laws of nature" governing our existence, the better we can anticipate their effects on us, and the more likely we are to produce an adaptive strategy for long-term survival with a high quality, democratic life for all. We cannot afford to ignore the dynamic ecological forces that have shaped our evolution and control our future options.

Human Effects on Ecosystems—Humans cause many disturbances to ecosystems. The more humans dominate an ecosystem, the more dramatic the disturbances. If disturbances are too profound, the relationship becomes unsustainable.

The living components in Jackson Hole—the plants and animals—have been significantly affected by human presence in this century. Most dramatically, considerable areas of habitat have been taken over by humans displacing plants and animals. The riparian and aquatic communities and their many inhabitants, including Snake River cutthroat trout,

Table 8.1 World population growth from year 0 to stabilization
(from United Nations 1996, data from the Population Division, Department of Economic and Social Information and Policy Analysis)

Year	Population (in billions)
0	0.30
1000	0.31
1250	0.40
1500	0.50
1750	0.79
1800	0.98
1850	1.26
1900	1.65
1910	1.75
1920	1.86
1930	2.07
1940	2.30
1950	2.52
1960	3.02
1970	3.70
1980	4.45
1990	5.30
2000	6.23
2025	8.47
2050	10.02
2100	11.19
2150	11.54
Stabilization (just after 2200)	11.6

have been affected. The meadow communities in the valley floor have been usurped by agricultural activities *(figure 8.6)*. Only one-sixth of historic elk winter range remains in the valley in southern Jackson Hole because of encroachment and associated disturbances.

Many alien plant and animal species have been introduced into the ecosystem—some intentionally, others accidentally. There are now 117 exotic plant species in Grand Teton National Park and surrounding areas in Teton County. This number is 63 percent higher than in 1968, and it is expected to increase in future years. Mountain goats, Norway rats, house mice, domestic livestock and pets, European starlings, and house sparrows have all been introduced. Aquatic communities have been hard hit by introductions. Exotic amphibians, like bullfrogs, have been introduced into Kelly Warm Springs. Tropical aquarium fish have been released into some warm springs.

Non-native brown trout, rainbow trout, brook trout, and lake trout have been put into many streams and lakes. Exotic insect introductions probably have occurred. The most troubling exotics are diseases such as giardia, brucellosis, and bovine tuberculosis, all introduced to the valley by livestock. These exotics have many harmful ecological impacts. They compete with native species, prey on them, hybridize with them, and transmit diseases. The financial costs of eradicating them are high. Often called "biological pollution," exotics are leading to homogenization and impoverishment of biotic communities.

Energy flows are disrupted and diverted away from native components and toward humans and our crops. Biogeochemical cycles are disrupted, and materials are deflected from native organisms into human systems. Four examples of human disruption of biogeochemical cycling worldwide affect us here in Jackson Hole.

Table 8.2 Annual worldwide introduction of selected toxic elements into the environment from natural and manmade sources. Natural sources include dust, volcanoes, forest fires, vegetation, and sea salt. Human sources include mining; smelting, iron production, and other industrial activities; waste incineration; phosphorus fertilizer production; and combustion of coal, wood, and petroleum.
(from B.L. Turner II et al., 1990, The earth as transformed by human action, *Cambridge University Press*)

Elements (in thousands of metric tons)	Natural sources	Manmade sources
Arsenic	7.80	23.6
Cadmium	0.96	7.3
Lead	18.60	449.0
Selenium	0.40	1.1
Mercury	0.16	1.8

First, heavy metals (such as lead), pesticides, and other toxins harm nearly all living organisms including humans *(table 8.2)*. The damage caused by these elements or compounds is magnified as they accumulate in higher trophic levels of food webs. Humans and other species at the top of food chains suffer. We sometimes overload or redirect material flows (such as siltation and sewer discharge into waterways), which disrupts the natural course of ecological events. Burning wood and fossil fuels in winter, mining, fertilizing crops, and spraying pesticides all release toxins into the ecosystem.

Second, the ozone shield surrounding the earth is being damaged by human activities. This layer of ozone in the atmosphere about 6 to 10 miles high protects all life from damaging ultraviolet radiation from sunlight. Loss of this shield causes cancer and genetic damage. A one-percent loss in the ozone layer causes a two-percent increase in ultraviolet light striking the earth's surface and a five- to seven-percent increase in skin cancer in humans. In recent decades humans have been releasing chemicals into the

8.6 *Crops have replaced meadow communities in Jackson Hole since the early days of settlement.*

atmosphere—chlorofluorocarbons in refrigerants, industrial solvents, and spray propellants; carbon tetrachloride, a cleaning agent and industrial solvent; and nitric oxides, waste products from fossil fuels. These interact with the ozone and destroy it. Over the last few decades, global levels of ozone have dropped about forty percent over Antarctica and two to six percent over the United States. Even though international agreements are trying to reduce emission of harmful chemicals, it will take decades before the ozone layer returns to normal, if at all.

A third disruption of biogeochemical cycling is global warming. Carbon dioxide in the atmosphere serves to retain heat, keeping the planet warm and livable. But humans have been adding excessive amounts of carbon dioxide and other gases to the atmosphere for the last couple hundred years—largely from the burning of fossil fuels. There is widespread concern that the planet may become too warm. A warmer planet will change global wind and climate patterns, which would have significant consequences for all life, including our own. Effects in Jackson Hole and the Greater Yellowstone Ecosystem could be significant—possibly drying and shifting seasonal patterns of precipitation.

Fourth is acid precipitation. The release of sulfur dioxide and nitrogen dioxides into the atmosphere over the last century has caused the acid content or pH of precipitation to fall below 5.6 in some areas. These compounds come from internal combustion engines, agricultural fertilizers, and coal-burning electric-generation plants. Acid rain causes organisms in aquatic systems to become highly stressed, especially if the pH falls below 4.0. Acid rain's effects in terrestrial systems are more complicated, causing leaching of mineral soils,

for example. This phenomenon ultimately harms people because it damages crops, pollutes drinking water, and corrodes metals, paints, and concrete. Preliminary data show that Surprise and Amphitheater Lakes, among others, are potentially at risk of acid rain effects.

Jackson Hole is affected by these four kinds of biogeochemical cycle disruptions largely because of human activities farther west and south in the United States and elsewhere on the planet. The valley is intimately interconnected to all other ecosystems making up the biosphere—directly or indirectly. We are not isolated nor insulated in Jackson Hole, economically or ecologically, from what happens elsewhere on the planet.

Humans also modify natural processes in the Jackson Hole ecosystem. We have seen that natural fire, insect outbreaks, earth movements, floods, and other processes created conditions that support diverse communities in the landscape. Humans have modified the rates and scales of many of these natural processes. We put out fires, apply pesticides to insect outbreaks, dam rivers, plow and irrigate certain biotic communities, cut forests, graze livestock in many plant communities, and fertilize the soil and let it blow away. Individually and cumulatively, these human activities affect how the ecosystem functions in terms of its components, energy flows, and biogeochemical cycles. Often the full impacts of these effects on ecosystems are little appreciated.

Ecosystems and human disruptions of them are not only more complex than we first thought but probably more complex than we can ever know. Interactions among thousands of components keep ecosystems in a state of dynamic equilibrium, popularly

called "the balance of nature." Two or more components may interact synergistically, that is, their combined effect may be greater than the sum of their individual effects. Conversely, they may interact antagonistically and partially or wholly cancel each other's effects. Ecosystems may become overloaded and break down. Responses of ecosystem components and processes may be characterized by "time lags" and "overshoots." In other words, the effects of changing the nature or level of interactions between components may not be felt for years or decades (such as nitrogen fertilizers currently damaging the upper atmosphere). By the time adverse effects first become known, the ecosystem may no longer be able to return to a more stable and desirable equilibrium. Because of these phenomena, the role of random events, and other complexities, it is impossible to predict the effects of humans' impacts on natural ecosystems except in simple cases. Intuitive, common sense approaches often fail to appreciate, understand, or "tinker" successfully with these complex ecological processes.

Since we may never completely understand how all ecosystem components are interconnected, we would be wise to operate in the ecosystem with a sense of humility and creative cooperation rather than blind domination. In the past, all we needed to do when an area was depleted or damaged was move to a new area and start over. But today there are no new areas left.

TOWARD A SUSTAINABLE FUTURE

Humanity is facing a global crisis. We are totally dependent upon the biosphere's ecological integrity for our own well-being, yet we are currently using the environment in ways and at levels that are damaging the biosphere. Our current situation is not sustainable. Unsustainability is rooted in our cultural foundations in religion, science, and economics. Many scholars believe that the development of western cultures created a process of ever-modernizing, open-ended material change. Accompanying this have been changes in expectations and demands, the almost-instantaneous application of new knowledge, loss of traditions, a globalizing world economy, and a strong future orientation. What needs to be done now is to retain the best and most beneficial aspects of our culture while minimizing the harmful effects of the current modernization.

Public policy is slowly but increasingly responding to this perceived challenge. There is growing discussion worldwide about sustainability, although locally the debate is just beginning. A hundred years ago in Jackson Hole people were much less buffered against environmental extremes such as cold temperatures, heavy snows, and a brief, unpredictable growing season (*figure 8.7*). Many technological and material advances have since made our lives more comfortable, more predictable, and more secure. Today the environment matters to us in very different ways than it did in olden days. The linkages between the environment and human prosperity are of growing import to the public and governments. Discussion is taking form in Teton County about how to plan for land uses, how to accommodate tourists, and what uses are appropriate

for the forest and parks. At the heart of the debate is the notion of sustainability or sustainable conservation.

Sustainability Concept—The sustainability agenda is not simply or primarily to promote environmental issues as conventionally understood, but to integrate environmental or ecological concerns with future human development. Like its opposite, the concept of sustainability has roots going back to the very foundations of western civilization. In this century, there have been many books, events, meetings, and laws addressing sustainability in one way or another. Its modern incarnation goes back about two decades. One of the most important events was the publication in 1980, through cooperation of many governments and concerned groups, of the *World Conservation Strategy*. The aims of the strategy, which was subtitled "living resource conservation for sustainable development," were to maintain essential ecological processes and life-support systems, preserve genetic diversity, and ensure the sustainable use of species and ecosystems. Since that time we have learned much about environmental threats and the difficulties of development, and there have been many dramatic changes in world governments—all of which have had a strong impact on "globalizing" the environment.

These events led to the Brundtland Report from the World Commission on Environment and Development in 1987, which gave us the definition of *sustainable development* now in wide usage. Sustainable development is that which meets the needs of the present without compromising the ability of future generations to meet their own needs. This idea contains two key concepts—"meeting needs" and "limitations." Like the concept of justice, sustainability does not have a precise, universal definition to which all people

subscribe, nor is one needed in order to make progress. Like justice, sustainability is an ideal worth striving for, and it is an idea whose time has come.

The forum for giving the Brundtland Report practical meaning was the 1992 World Conference on Environment and Development held in Rio de Janeiro, Brazil—commonly called the Rio Conference. About 18,000 people attended and over 400,000 more visited the conference—clear evidence of the worldwide concern about sustainability and sustainable development. The Rio Conference was by far the strongest statement ever made about the aim of the human enterprise. International agreements were reached among 179 countries, including the *Rio Declaration on Environment and Development*, *Agenda 21—Programme of Action for Sustainable Development*, *Statement for Forest Principles*, *Framework Convention on Climate Change*, and *Convention on Biological Diversity*.

Countries throughout the world have set up oversight committees to develop national strategies to achieve sustainability. Some countries in fact have had such plans in place for several years now. The United States has also been active. In 1996 the President's Council on Sustainable Development produced a document called *Sustainable America: A new consensus for prosperity, opportunity, and a healthy environment for the future*. The challenge is to give meaning to the concept of sustainability by applying it practically and meaningfully in local settings. The goal of a healthy, biologically diverse, and sustainable environment is in everyone's interest—it is the common interest. However, clarifying and securing the common interest are not necessarily straightforward processes.

Searching for Sustainability in Jackson Hole—In the 1970s during the first major debate over Teton County's land use plan, Jackson Hole resident Jack de Golia wrote a letter to the editor about the problem of finding the common interest:

Land use planning, national forests and parks, and endangered species studies are remedies for excesses of the 19th century idea that an individual could do whatever he pleased, which is not a constitutional right but a social attitude that was reflected in law. But the frontier closed in 1890. And there has been a growing concern since then that without some regulation, an individual could threaten the freedom of the mass of individuals by considering only what was good for himself.

Monopolies, abuses of labor, overgrazing, and destruction of wildlife and wildlife habitat have come to be viewed as threats to all of us. In providing for the "general welfare," Congress and other elected bodies have reflected the public concern that the actions of one man should not selfishly destroy something of value to all.

There are too many of us nowadays . . . for Teton County to be released from all regulation of use. So while some may miss the days before 1912 when you could walk or ride across what is now the Elk Refuge, when you could hunt anywhere in the valley for anything, or when you could homestead anywhere on public land, we must realize we had to trade something for those days. We have traded the ability of one person to do anything anywhere for the ability of a huge number of people to do quite a lot and still not destroy the place that drew them here in the first place.

People's "sense of place" and strong personal attachment to the place where they live produces a caring attitude in a community's residents. Three things

8.7 *Deep snows periodically affect the valley's residents.*

are needed to nurture a sense of place and an attachment to place—the practice of social and cultural traditions, traditional patterns of rural, suburban, and urban development, and the existence of a healthy natural environment. In Jackson Hole all three have changed rapidly and dramatically in recent years,

and as a result we have suffered a loss of attachment and caring.

We must find ways to measure and understand our quality of life in Jackson Hole. "Quality of life" is often equated with standard of living, per capita income, or material wealth. While this is an important measure of our well-being, it is by no means the sole indicator of the quality of our lives. People value a lot more than money—they cherish family and community, education, health, politeness and deference, a clean environment, the ability to make a good living, and having a say in what happens to the community and the environment. A suitable index of quality should include all these values that are indicative of the human condition. For Jackson Hole, such an index might include measures of littering, fishing, hunting, backcountry use and impacts, tourist volume and visiting patterns, traffic congestion in town, crime rates, status of families in the valley, health care problems and services, community stability, waste disposal problems, wildlife habitat quality, crowding, water rationing, air quality, and more. Deciding which criteria to use will be a challenge, but if citizens know what is actually happening to the things they value, then we might all come to share a common "map" of our community— where it has been and where it seems to be going. This kind of measuring and monitoring activity would be a good

step toward our collective search for the common interest.

Progress Toward Sustainability—How has the effort to achieve sustainability proceeded in the region? Let's look briefly at two cases where we did not live up to our potential for problem solving. These examples illustrate how we have fallen short, but both offer valuable insights and lessons on how to succeed in future efforts to achieve sustainability. Then we will look at three cases where significant progress is being made.

First, in 1987 the U.S. Forest Service and the National Park Service launched a joint coordination and planning process for the Greater Yellowstone region, commonly called the "Vision exercise," and produced a draft document in 1990 and a final in 1991. From the beginning, it faced strong opposition from many fronts, including traditional commodity extraction industries, and indifference from others, including conservationists. The process was perceived by many as a policy failure. It did not lead to any formal policy changes. Critics charged

that the agencies had unclear objectives, that they were out of touch with a highly politicized operating environment, that they miscalculated foreseeable public reaction, and that they deliberately used vague language to preserve their discretion and minimize accountability. It seems clear that if we are to achieve regional sustainability, we must go about it quite differently than the conventional approach unsuccessfully tried by the agencies in this case.

Second, efforts to write a management plan for Jackson Hole's bison have dragged on for more than a decade without producing an acceptable outcome that enjoys broad public support (see *Caldera* 1996 for a review of this issue). The proposed management plan is not factually well grounded nor does it reflect majority values in the community. The debate centers on how many bison to allow to roam in Jackson Hole, what techniques are acceptable (and compatible with management of other resources) to maintain the herd at the chosen level, and how to prevent and mitigate conflicts (real or perceived)

Bison

with humans. Although the real conflicts appear to be negligible, a powerful minority perceives a significant problem in the possible transmission of brucellosis (a disease introduced to wildlife by livestock) from wild bison to domestic cattle. All these questions are being asked in the context of fierce conflicts over the management of bison in neighboring Yellowstone National Park.

Both these public policy efforts displayed a host of weaknesses and rigidities that led to failures in the search for a common interest. The participants in both cases seemed unaware of the likely pitfalls in advance and thus made little effort to avoid them. The process of deciding public policy can be blinded, for example, by failures in intelligence, that is, by not gathering, assessing, and using ecological or other kinds of knowledge appropriately. Sometimes problems are weakly analyzed or poorly defined; key issues, for instance, may not be addressed. The process may be blocked by various kinds of rigidities, such as narrow ideology. Or it can be distorted by power and wealth in ways that serve the few and disregard the majority. Often the context of the problem is misunderstood—including social, political, economic, historical, and symbolic elements. In many policy arenas public input is limited and formulaic. Finally, the recurrence of many of these problems suggests that people and organizations are not learning as much as they could from their past experiences.

These kinds of weaknesses—which are common in all kinds of public policy issues—do not have to be repeated in debates about sustainability in Teton County. They are predictable and avoidable, regardless of the form and substance of the debate. First, with certain complex issues like sustainability—particularly when shifting emphasis away from traditional uses—we must state our purposes explicitly and put forth clear objectives for implementing change. Second, we must specify practical mechanisms to deal with problems that might impede our goal. Third, we should assess the social, organizational, political, and economic impacts that might result from our decisions. We must also analyze how people and organizations might respond to these real—or, more importantly, perceived—changes prior to their implementation. Fourth, we should initiate a partnership with government so that public values—despite their broad range and often conflicting nature—will not only be incorporated but help drive the effort to find the common interest. Fifth, active educational efforts can greatly benefit the process by informing everyone—the public, the agencies, and various interfaces between agencies and levels of government—about the issues. Such efforts will enable everyone to participate in meaningful ways in problem solving and decision making. And sixth, decision makers may benefit from additional training and experience to avoid well known pitfalls. There are conceptual frameworks and methods available for dealing with public policy issues.

I would like to cite three positive examples of progress toward sustainability in Jackson Hole. First is the Teton County comprehensive land use planning effort. In 1989 and 1990, the town and county began to gather information on the community and county, the many growing problems it faced, and what to do about them. Community groups, workshops, neighborhood meetings, and town and county elections were forums for this search. Key issues in the debate were population growth, commercial development, community character, natural, scenic, and wildlife resources, afford-able housing, open space, ranching and agriculture, and balance in the community (rather than domination by lodging and resorts). Through this process the community set goals for planning.

In 1994 Teton County adopted a Comprehensive Land Use Plan. It is a working specification of the common interest for the time being. Although the plan goes far in balancing diverse political, economic, and environmental interests and restricts some negative impacts and unsustainable practices, it is a compromise that falls short of providing complete protection for many valuable natural, scenic, and cultural resources in Jackson Hole. Future planning iterations must still address wildlife and water quality protection, maintenance of community stability, and low cost housing, among other problems. Planning has been a major issue for over 20 years in Jackson Hole and no end is in sight. But this is as it should be: securing the common interest is a never-ending process of adaptation.

Second is the efforts of the Jackson Hole Conservation Alliance in the county planning process. This not-for-profit organization, created in the 1970s, promotes a human and natural community in balance. The Alliance notes that long-range, valley-wide planning may be our only hope for retaining the ecosystem's irreplaceable natural and scenic resources and a sense of community among its human inhabitants. Among its many activities, the Alliance works to show citizens of the Jackson Hole ecosystem that there are many practical things they can do to promote sustainable values. For example, the organization recently published a booklet that suggests ways to protect wildlife habitat when building and landscaping, it sponsored a public talk on alternative and recycled building mate-

rials, and it has conducted field trips to grizzly-occupied public lands to explore complex management issues. Other local organizations also contribute to this effort. The Jackson Hole Land Trust, for instance, purchases conservation easements and protects open space in the valley. The Northern Rockies Conservation Cooperative carries out broad-based problem solving through workshops, conferences, technical studies, and policy analyses.

Finally, a third positive illustration is the fact that discussions about sustainability are taking place in the Greater Yellowstone Ecosystem. This 19-million-acre region is one of the most ecologically intact temperate ecosystems left on the planet. But there are disagreements about how to use, manage, or protect the region. People promoting one set of interests want to continue traditional resource exploitation and year round tourism with minimal regard for the long-term sustainability of such practices. They appeal to the long-standing tradition of commerce, industry, and individualism as legitimate and reliable means of

enhancing regional economic prosperity and human welfare. Another set of interests, however, increasingly views that approach as serving primarily special, rather than common, interests. These people instead see a higher good in protecting regional natural resources and advancing the sustainability of Greater Yellowstone.

Ecosystem management is one of the approaches being promoted by this alliance of interests to remedy past and current management problems and achieve sustainability. Although not well defined at present, such an approach would integrate landscape management over much larger areas than has previously been done. It would seek to protect the things valued by a large number of people, not just a few people. If ecosystem management is to become a practical reality, it will require precedent-setting, interrelated changes in disciplinary specialties, professional norms, government agencies, academic involvement, management philosophies, and policies. Yellowstone, the first national park, could again be a model for the rest of

the world by developing a practicable policy of ecosystem management.

The debate over the sustainability of the Greater Yellowstone Ecosystem has taken a clear form in the last 15 years in numerous articles, publications, and meetings about mining, fires, wildlife, and many more issues. The debate is already paying off in tangible ways. First, it has changed the way people talk about the region, its values, its uses, and the state and federal agencies that manage a large part of it. The notion of sustainability lays out an attractive vision for the future and erodes the legitimacy of old, traditional practices and outlooks and the interests that support them.

Second, it has changed the allocation of responsibility (blame and credit) for the costs and benefits of traditional agency management and extractive uses. This shift in responsibility is obvious in the growing defensiveness of some interest groups and the perceived legitimacy and activism of others.

Third, the debate over sustainability has changed awareness of the significance of Jackson Hole and the

Greater Yellowstone Ecosystem among citizens, businesses, and politicians. Once considered merely a vacation spot, the region and its management now receive attention from the media, the public, scientific communities, and official circles at national and international levels.

Fourth, this new idea of sustainability has changed patterns of citizen mobilization. By bringing new values to the forefront, it has stimulated and channeled activism both within the agencies and outside. Organizations that promote sustainability are flourishing in terms of memberships, budgets, and staffs. The advocacy, analysis, and research focused on sustainability are leaching away the power of traditional commodity extraction interests, old management philosophies deeply rooted in government agency cultures and procedures, and customary business arrangements. The idea of sustainability is helping to build new coalitions based on mid- to long-term rather than short-term planning, cooperation rather than competition and conflict, and integration and synthesis rather than fragmentation. It is an idea that promises a great deal for ecological and human well-being, but its eventual success is contingent on the continued hard work of many people and organizations.

CONCLUSION

We humans have innumerable biological properties in common with other animals and even with plants. Our bodies are structures of living cells, tissues, and organs, all made up of molecules and atoms. Like other creatures, our bodies respond to chemical stimuli, light, heat, and pressure. Like other animals, we eat, digest, eliminate, respire, reproduce, and locomote. We

are as fully subject to nature's laws as any other animals and no more capable of permanently changing these laws than other animals. Humans live in biological communities and have an ecology. As British biologist J. B. S. Haldane noted, "I am a part of nature, and like other natural objects, from a lightning flash to a mountain range, I shall last out my time and then finish." We cannot ever afford to forget these aspects of our nature. A philosophical view of humanity that does not accept our biological and ecological nature is merely a fiction or a falsity. We are part of nature even though we have evolved particular adaptations, including richly varied cultures and myths that give some the illusion of independence from the natural environment.

Jackson Hole is a microcosm of many philosophical as well as practical problems, such as sustainability, that face communities worldwide. The political, environmental, and economic struggles common in Jackson Hole today are evidence of our attempts to forge a healthy, adaptive, sustainable worldview and way of life here. Our situation was characterized by the scientist and philosopher Jacob Bronowski, "And yet fifty years from now, if an understanding of man's origins, his evolution, his history, his progress is not the commonplace of the schoolbooks, we shall not exist. The commonplace of the schoolbooks of tomorrow is the adventure of today, and this is what we are engaged in."

We must consciously apply ecological principles if we are to live harmoniously within our limited environment, or, indeed, if we are ultimately to flourish and achieve sustainability. The choice is ours. Good will and good judgment will be needed. If we meet this challenge head on and if we can change to meet the demands of

a new situation with knowledge, imagination, and skill, we can have a rich and sustainable environment for ourselves and our posterity.

RECOMMENDED RESOURCES

Caldera: A journal of living in Jackson Hole. The Buffalo Jubilee Issue. No. 5, Fall 1996. P. O. Box 1540, Jackson WY 83001. 64 pp.

Clark, T. W., and S. C. Minta. 1994. *Greater Yellowstone's future: Prospects for ecosystem science, management, and policy.* Homestead Press, Moose, Wyoming. 160 pp.

Constanza, R., B. G. Norton, and B. D. Haskell, eds. 1992. *Ecosystem health: New goals for environmental management.* Island Press, Washington. 269 pp.

President's Council on Sustainble Development. 1996. *Sustainable America: A new consensus for prosperity, opportunity, and a healthy environment for the future.* U.S. Government Printing Office, Washington. 186 pp.

Wilson, E. O., ed. 1988. *Biodiversity.* National Academy Press, Washington. 521 pp.

References

Allan, E. B. 1973. *History of Teton National Forest*. Wyoming State Historical Society, Cheyenne. 376 pp.

Allen, M. V. 1981. *Early Jackson Hole*. Press Room Printing, Inc., Redding, California. 400 pp.

Alexander, R. D. 1971. *The search for an evolutionary philosophy of man*. Proceedings of the Royal Society. *Victoria* 84:99-120.

Anderson, D. D. 1958. *The elk of Jackson Hole, Wyoming*. Wyoming Game and Fish Bulletin 10: 1-182.

Baker, R. G. 1970. *Pollen sequences from Late Quaternary sediments in Yellowstone Park*. Science 168: 1449-1450.

Bartlett, R. A. 1985. *Yellowstone: A wilderness besieged*. University of Arizona Press, Tuscon. 436 pp.

Baxter, G. T., and J. R. Simon. 1970. *Wyoming fishes*. Wyoming Game and Fish Department, Cheyenne. 168 pp.

Beetle, A. A. 1961. *Range survey in Teton County, Wyoming, Part I: Ecology of range resources*. University of Wyoming Agricultural Experiment Station Bulletin 376R:1-42.

Begon, M., J. L. Harper, and C. R. Townsend. 1986. *Ecology: Individuals, populations, and communities*. Sinauer Associates, Sunderland, Massachusetts. 876 pp.

Bender, S. J. 1977. *Archaeological investigations in the northern Tetons: A study in high country adaptations*. Unpublished Manuscript. 25 pp.

Betts, R. B. 1978. *Along the ramparts of the Tetons: The saga of Jackson Hole, Wyoming*. Colorado Associated University Press, Boulder. 249 pp.

Beveridge, W. I. B. 1950. *The art of scientific investigation*. Vintage Books, New York. 239 pp.

Blackstone, D. L., Jr. 1971. *Traveler's guide to the geology of Wyoming*. Wyoming Geological Survey, Laramie. 90 pp.

Bonney, O. H., and L. G. Bonney. 1977. *Field book: The Teton Range and the Gros Ventre Range*. Swallow Press, Chicago. 263 pp.

Bormann, F. H., and G. E. Likens. 1979. *Pattern and process in a forested ecosystem*. Springer-Verlag, New York. 253 pp.

Boulding, K. 1966. *The economics of the coming spaceship earth*. Pp. 3-14 in H. Jarrett, ed., Environmental quality in a growing economy. Johns Hopkins University Press and Resources for the Future, Baltimore.

Boulding, K. E. 1974. *What went wrong, if anything, since Copernicus?* Bulletin of the Atomic Scientist, June:17-23.

Boyce, M. S. 1989. *Elk management in North America: The Jackson herd*. Cambridge Press, Cambridge. 306 pp.

Brewer, R. 1988. *The science of ecology*. Saunders College Publishing, New York. 907 pp.

Bridger-Teton National Forest. 1989. *Bridger-Teton National Forest: Final environmental impact statement—summary*. Jackson, Wyoming. 24 pp.

Brown, T., Jr., 1983. *Tom Brown's field guide to nature observation and tracking*. Berkeley Books, New York. 282 pp.

Bruhn, J. G. 1972. *The ecological crises and the work ethic*. Aldine Publishing Company, Chicago. 347 pp.

Brunner, R. D., and T. W. Clark. 1997. *A practice-based approach to ecosystem management*. Conservation Biology 11:48-58.

Camenzind, F. J. 1976. *Coyotes: a new generation*. Persimmon Hill 6:12-19.

Campbell, T. M., III. 1991. *Winter ecology of the Gros Ventre Buttes mule deer herd, Jackson Hole, Wyoming:* Winter 1989-1990. Biota Research and Consulting, Jackson, Wyoming. Progress Report XI:1-37 + appendices.

Carson, R. 1963. *Silent spring*. Houghton Mifflin, Boston. 245 pp.

Cary, M. 1917. *Life zone investigations in Wyoming*. U.S.D.A., Bureau Biological Survey, North Amerecan Fauna No 42:1-95.

Casey, D., and T. W. Clark. 1996. *Tales of the wolf: Fifty-one stories of wolf encounters in the wild*. Homestead Press, Moose, Wyoming. 294 pp.

Clark, T. W. 1973. *Local distribution and interspecies interactions in microtines, Grand Teton National Park, Wyoming*. Great Basin Naturalist 33:205-217.

Clark, T. W. 1989. *Conservation biology of the black-footed ferret Mustela nigripes*. Wildlife Preservation Trust Special Scientific Report 3:1-175.

Clark, T. W., and T. M. Campbell III. 1981. *Winter ecology and migratory movements of the Gros Ventre Buttes mule deer herd, Jackson Hole, Wyoming*. Biota Research and Consulting, Jackson, Wyoming. Progress Report I:1-73.

Clark, T. W., and T. M. Campbell, III. 1981. *Botanical and wildlife data for the Spring Creek Ranch, East Gros Ventre Butte, Teton County, Wyoming*. Biota Research and Consulting, Jackson, Wyoming. 196 pp.

Clark, T. W., E. Anderson, C. Douglas, and M. Strickland. 1987. *Martes americana*. Mammalian Species 289:1-8.

Clark, T. W., and M. R. Stromberg. 1987. *Mammals in Wyoming*. University of Kansas Press, Lawrence. 314 pp.

Clark, T. W., A. H. Harvey, R. D. Dorn, D. L. Genter, and C. R. Croves. 1989a. *Rare, sensitive, and threatened species of the Greater Yellowstone Ecosystem*. Northern Rockies Conservation Cooperative, Montana Natural Heritage Program, The Nature Conservancy, and Mountain West Environmental Services. Jackson, Wyoming. 153 pp.

Clark, T. W., T. M. Campbell III, and T. N. Hauptman. 1989b. *Demographic characteristics of American marten population in Jackson Hole, Wyoming.* Great Basin Naturalist 49:587-596.

Clark, T. W., R. M. Warneke, and G. C. George. 1990. *Management and conservation of small populations.* Pp. 1-18 in T. W. Clark, and J. H. Seebeck, eds., Management and conservation of small populations. Chicago Zoological Society, Brookfield.

Clark, T. W., and S. C. Minta. 1994. *Greater Yellowstone's future: Prospects for ecosystem science, management, and policy.* Homestead Press, Moose, Wyoming. 160 pp.

Clark, T. W., A. P. Curlee, and R. P. Reading. 1996. *Crafting effective solutions to the large carnivore conservation problem.* Conservation Biology 10:949-963.

Cole, L. C. 1964. *The impending emergence of ecological thought.* BioScience 14:30-32.

Cole, G. F. 1969. *The elk of Grand Teton and southern Yellowstone National Parks.* Fauna of National Parks, Fauna Series 8:1-128.

Commoner, B. 1971. *The closing circle: Man, nature, and technology.* Knopf, New York. 343 p.

Commoner, B. 1976. The poverty of power: Energy and the economic crises. Knopf, New York. 314 p.

Constanza, R., B. G. Norton, and B. D. Haskell, eds. 1992. *Ecosystem health: New goals for environmental management.* Island Press, Washington. 269 pp.

Cook, R. S., ed. 1993. *Ecological issues on reintroducing wolves into Yellowstone National Park, Scientific Monograph* NPLS/NRYELL/NRSM-93/22:1-328.

Craighead, F. C., Jr. 1994. *For everything there is a season: The sequence of natural events in the Grand Teton-Yellowstone area.* Falcon Press, Helena, Montana. 206 pp.

Craighead, F. C., Jr. 1951. *A biological and economic evaluation of coyote predation.* New York Zoological Society and Conservation Foundation. 23 pp.

Craighead, J. J., F. C. Craighead, and R. J. Davis. 1963. *A field guide to Rocky Mountain wildflowers.* Houghton Mifflin Co., Boston. 277 p.

Craighead, J. J., J. R. Varney, and F. C. Craighead. 1974. *A population analysis of the Yellowstone grizzly bears.* Montana Forest and Conservation Experiment Station Bulletin 40:1-20.

Craighead, K. No Date. *Large mammals of Yellowstone and Teton National Parks: How to know them—where to see them.* Walker Press, Paris, Ontario. 31 pp.

Crandall, H. 1978. *Grand Teton: The story behind the scenery.* KC Publications, Las Vegas. 48 pp.

Cronon, W., G. Miles, and J. Gitlin. 1992. *Under an open sky: Rethinking America's western past.* W.W. Norton and Company, New York. 354 pp.

Daly, H. E. 1971. *Toward a stationary state economy.* Pp. 68-84 in J. Harte and R. H. Socolow, eds., Patient earth. Holt, Rinehart, and Winston, New York.

Daly, H. E. 1977. *Steady-state economics.* W.H. Freeman & Co., San Francisco. 185 pp.

Daubenmire, R. F. 1943. *Vegetational zonation in the Rocky Mountains.* Botany Review 9:325-393.

Debinski, D. 1996. *Using satellite data to support field work.* Yellowstone Science 4(3):2-5.

de Golia, J. 1989. *Fire: The story behind a force of nature.* KC Publications, Inc., Las Vegas. 47 pp.

Despain, D. G. 1990. *Yellowstone vegetation: Consequences of environment and history in a natural setting.* Roberts Rinehart, Boulder, Colorado. 239 pp.

Dorn, R. D. 1986. *The Wyoming landscape, 1805-1878.* Mountain West Publishing, Cheyenne. 94 pp.

Dorn, R. D. 1988. *Vascular plants of Wyoming.* Mountain West Publishing, Cheyenne. 339 pp.

Dovers, S. R. 1996. *Policy process for sustainability.* Ph.D. Thesis, Australian National University, Canberra. 362 pp.

Dubos, R. 1968. *So human an animal.* Charles Scribner's Sons, New York. 267 pp.

Duffy, K., and D. Wile. 1995. *Teton trails: A guide to the trails of Grand Teton National Park.* Grand Teton Natural History Association, Moose, Wyoming. 163 pp.

Emlen, J. M. 1973. *Ecology: An evolutionary approach.* AddisonWesley, Reading, Massachusetts. 493 pp.

Environmental Pollution Panel of President's Science Advisory Committee. 1965. *Restoring the quality of our environment.* U.S. GPO, Washington. 317 pp.

Ferguson, G. 1996. *The Yellowstone wolves: The first year.* Falcon Press, Helena. 174 pp.

Fischer, H. 1995. *Wolf wars: The remarkable inside story of the restoration of wolves to Yellowstone.* Falcon Press, Helena. 182 pp.

Fitzsimmons, A. K. 1976. *National Parks: The dilemma of development.* Science 191:440-444.

Ford Foundation. 1974. *A time to choose America's energy future.* Ballinger Publ. Co., Cambridge. 511 pp.

Forrest, L. R. 1988. *Field guide to tracking animals in snow.* Stackpole Books, Harrisburg, Pennsylvania. 213 pp.

Forman, R. T. T., and M. Godron. 1986. *Landscape ecology.* John Wiley and Sons, New York. 619 pp.

Fowells, H. A. 1965. *Silvics of forest trees of the United States.* Agricultural Handbook. U.S.D.A. 762 pp.

Fox, R. 1970. *The cultural animal.* Pp. 31-42 in J. F. Eisenberg, ed., Man and beast. Smithsonian Symposium, Washington.

Francis, T. 1992. *Yellowstone wildlife: A watcher's guide.* Northwood Press, Minoqua, Wisconsin. 96 pp.

Fritts, S. H., E. E. Bangs, J. A. Fontaine, W. G. Brewster, and J. F. Gore. 1995. *Restoring wolves to the northern Rocky Mountains of the United States.* Pp. 107-126 in L. N. Carbyn, S. H. Fritts, and D. R. Seip, eds, Ecology and conservation of wolves in a changing world. Canadian Circumpolar Institute, University of Alberta, Edmonton.

Frixell, F. 1995. *The Tetons: Interpretations of a mountain landscape.* Grand Teton Natural History Association, Moose, Wyoming. 77 pp.

Geist, V. 1963. *On the behaviour of North American Moose (Alces alces andersoni Peterson 1950) in British Columbia.* Behaviour 20:377-416.

Gilmore, J. 1991. *Welcome to Grand Teton National Park: An explosion of life and color.* Grand Teton Natural History Association, Moose, Wyoming. 12 pp.

Gilmore, J. 1993. *Wildlife legacy: The National Elk Refuge.* Backwater Publications, Moose, Wyoming. 22 pp.

Glick, D., M. Carr, and B. Harting, eds. 1991. *An environmental profile of the Greater Yellowstone Ecosystem.* Greater Yellowstone Coalition, Bozeman, Montana. 132 pp.

Golley, F. B. 1972. *Energy flux in ecosystems.* Pp. 61-90 in J.A. Weins, ed., Ecosystem structure and function. Oregon State Universtity Press, Corvallis.

Golley, R. B. 1993. *A history of ecosystem concept in ecology: More than the sum of the parts.* Yale University Press, New Haven. 254 pp.

Good, J. M.,. and K. L. Pierce. 1996. *Interpreting the landscape: Recent and ongoing geology of Grand Teton and Yellowstone National Parks.* Grand Teton Natural History Association, Moose, Wyoming. 58 pp.

Grand Teton National Park. 1986. *Natural resources management plan and environmental assessment.* Moose, Wyoming. 459 pp.

Grand Teton National Park. 1996. *Snake River management plan: Grand Teton National Park.* Moose, Wyoming. 68 pp + appendices.

Greater Yellowstone Coalition and The Wilderness Society. 1993. *County economic profiles of the Greater Yellowstone Region.* Greater Yellowstone Coalition, Bozeman, Montana. 207 pp.

Greater Yellowstone Coordinating Committee. 1987. *An aggregation of national park and national forest management plans.* GYCC, Billings. 322 pp. + maps.

Gruell, G. E. 1973. *An ecological evaluation of Big Game Ridge* (Teton Wilderness). U.S.D.A., Forest Service, Bridger-Teton National Forest, Jackson, Wyoming. 62 pp.

Gruell, G. E. 1976. *Wildlife inventory of Jackson planning unit, Teton National Forest, Wyoming.* Unpublished Mansucript. 26 pp.

Gruell, G. E. and L. L. Loope. 1974. *Relationships among aspen, fire, and ungulate browsing in Jackson Hole, Wyoming.* U.S.D.A. Forest Service. 33 pp.

Gunderson, L. H., C. S. Holling, and S. S. Light, eds. 1995. *Barriers and bridges to the renewal of ecosystems and institutions.* Columbia University Press, New York. 593 pp.

Hagen, H. 1954. *A fishing guide to Jackson Hole.* Pioneer Printing Co., Cheyenne. 82 pp.

Haines, A. L., ed. 1955. *Osborne Russell's journal of a trapper (1834-1843).* University of Nebraska Press, Lincoln. 207 pp.

Haines, A. L. 1977. *The Yellowstone story.* Colorado Associated University Press, Boulder. Vol. I:1-385 and Vol II:1-543.

Halfpenny, J. 1986. *A field guide to mammal tracking in western America.* Johnson Publishing Company, Boulder, Colorado. 164 pp.

Halfpenny, J. C., and D. Thompson. 1996. *Discovering Yellowstone wolves: Watcher's guide.* A Naturalist's World, Gardiner, Montana. 61 pp.

Hardin, G. 1959. *Nature and man's fate.* Mentor Books., New York. 320 pp.

Hardin, G. 1973. *Exploring new ethics for survival: Voyage of the spaceship* Beagle. Pelican Press, Baltimore. 273 pp.

Harting, A., and D. Glick. 1994. *Sustaining Greater Yellowstone, a blueprint for the future.* Greater Yellowstone Coalition, Bozeman, Montana. 222 pp.

Harvey, A. 1994. *The aliens among us: Introduced species in the Greater Yellowstone Ecosystem.* Northern Rockies Conservation Cooperative, Jackson, Wyoming. NRCC News 7:4--5,7.

Hayden, E. W. 1992. *From trapper to tourist in Jackson Hole.* Grand Teton Natural History Association, Moose, Wyoming. 71 pp.

Hayden, P. S. 1969. *Jackson Lake limnological investigations.* National Park Service Progress Report, Moose, Wyoming. 69 pp.

Heilbroner, R. L. 1974. *An inquiry into the human prospect.* W. W. Norton, New York. 150 pp.

Houston, D. B. 1968. *The Shiras moose in Jackson Hole, Wyoming.* Grand Teton Natural History Society, Technical Bulletin 1:1-110.

Houston, D. B. 1971. *Ecosystems of national parks.* Science 172:648-651.

Houston, D. B. 1973. *Wildfires in northern Yellowstone National Park.* Ecology 54:111-117.

Huidekoper, V. 1978. *The early days in Jackson Hole.* Colorado Associated University Press, Boulder. 129 pp.

Iltis, H. H., O. L. Loucks, and P. Andrews. 1970. *Criteria for an optimum human environment.* Bulletin of the Atomic Scientists XXVI:2-6.

International Union for the Conservation of Nature and Natural Resources. 1991. *Caring for the earth: A strategy for sustainable living.* IUCN, Gland, Switzerland. 165 pp.

Jackson Hole Alliance for Responsible Planning. 1995. *Welcome to the neighborhood: 9 ways builders & homeowners can protect wildlife in the Jackson Hole area.* Jackson, Wyoming. 10 pp.

Jackson Hole Alliance for Responsible Planning. no date. *Creating a community in balance: An overview of the county land use plan.* Jackson, Wyoming. 10 pp.

Janovy, J., Jr. 1985. *On becoming a biologist.* Harper and Row, NewYork. 160 pp.

Jeffrey, D. 1989. *Yellowstone: The great fires of 1988.* National Geographic, February:252-273.

Keiter, R. B., and M. S. Boyce. 1991. *The Greater Yellowstone ecosystem.* Yale University Press, New Haven. 428 pp.

Kendeigh, S. G. 1965. *The ecology of man, the animal.* BioScience 15:521-523.

Kennedy, P. 1993. *Preparing for the twenty-first century.* Vintage Books, New York. 428 pp.

Klein, W. H., L. E. Stipe, and L. V. Frandsen. 1972. *How damaging is a mountain pine beetle infestation?* U.S.D.A. Forest Service, Timber Management, Ogden, Utah. 29 pp.

Kormondy, E. J. 1969. *Concepts in ecology.* Prentice-Hall, Englewoods Cliffs, New Jersey. 219 pp.

Kroger, R. L. 1967. *A study of the classification and ecology of the aquatic invertebrates of the Snake River, Grand Teton National Park.* M. S. Thesis, University of Wyoming, Laramie. 161 pp.

Knight, D. H. 1994. *Mountains and plains: The ecology of Wyoming landscapes.* Yale University Press, New Haven. 338 pp.

Koch, E. D., and C. R. Peterson. 1995. *Amphibians and reptiles of Yellowstone and Grand Teton National Parks.* University of Utah Press, Salt Lake City. 188 pp.

Lacy, R. C., and T. W. Clark. 1993. *Simulation modeling of American marten* (Martes americana) *populations: Vulnerability to extinction.* Great Basin Naturalist 53:282-292.

Larson, L. L., and H. H. Larson. 1988. *Grand Teton photographer's guide.* Earthwalk Press, Eureka, California. 44 pp.

Larson, T.A . 1984. *Wyoming: A history.* W.W. Norton and Company, New York. 198 pp.

Lasswell, H. D. 1971. *A pre-view to the policy sciences.* Elsevier, New York. 173 pp.

Lichtman, P., and T. W. Clark. 1994. *Rethinking the "vision" exercise in the Yellowstone Ecosystem.* Society and Natural Resources 7:459-478.

Limerick, P. N. 1987. *The legacy of conquest: The unbroken past of the American West.* W.W. Norton and Company, New York. 396 pp.

Leopold, A. 1949. *A Sand County almanac.* Ballantine Books, New York. 295 pp.

Longree, K. 1951. *A study on the microclimate of three areas in Jackson Hole Wildlife Park in relation to diurnal movements of elk to and from these areas.* Unpubl. Manuscript. 19 pp.

Loope, L. L. and G. E. Gruell. 1973. *The ecological role of fire in the Jackson Hole area, Northwestern Wyoming.* Journal of Quaternary Research. 3:425-443.

Love, C. M. 1975. *An archaeological survey of the Jackson Hole region, Wyoming.* The Wyoming Archaeologist 18:1-95.

Love, J. D., and J. C. Reed, Jr. 1968. *Creation of the Teton landscape.* Grand Teton Natural History Association, Moose, Wyoming. 120 pp.

Marshall, K. G., D. H. Knight, and W. J. Barmore, Jr. 1979. *An indexed and annotated bibliography on the ecology of Grand Teton National Park.* University of Wyoming and National Park Service Research Center, Grand Teton National Park, Moose, Wyoming. 106 pp.

Mattson, D. J., and J. J. Craighead. 1994. *The Yellowstone grizzly bear recovery program: Uncertain information, uncertain policy.* Pp. 101-132 in T. W. Clark, R. P. Reading, and A. L. Clarke, eds, Endangered species recovery: Finding the lessons, improving the process. Island Press, Washington.

Mattson, D. J., S. Herrero, R. G. Wright, and C. M. Pease. 1996. *Science and management of Rocky Mountain grizzly bears.* Conservation Biology 10:1,013-1,012.

Mayr, E. 1964. *Systematics and the origin of species.* Dover Publ., New York. 334 pp.

McKinley, D. 1964. *The new mythology of "man in nature."* Perspectives in Biology and Medicine 7:93-105.

McNaughton, S. J. and L. L. Wolf. 1975. *General ecology.* Holt, Rinehart, and Winston, New York. 710 pp.

McNulty, T. 1985. *Grand Teton National Park: Where lighting walks.* Woodlands Press, Englewood, Colorado. 72 pp.

Meadows, et al. 1972. *The limits of growth: A report for the Club of Rome's project on the predicament of mankind.* Universal Books, New York. 235 pp.

Meagher, M. M. 1973. *The bison of Yellowstone National Park.* National Park Service Monograph 1:1-161.

Medwar, P. B. 1979. *Advice to a young scientist.* Harper Colophon Books, New York. 109 pp.

Meffe, G. K., and C. R. Carroll. 1994. *Principles of conservation biology.* Sinauer Associates, Sunderland, Massachusetts. 600 pp.

Merkle, J. 1964. *Ecological studies in Holly Lake Cirque in the Teton Mountains, Wyoming.* Unpublished Manuscript. 18 pp.

Metillo, J. M. 1972. *Ecology primer.* Pendulum Press, New Haven. 246 pp.

Miller, G. T., Jr. 1975. *Living in the environment: Concepts, problems, and alternatives.* Wadsworth Publishing Company, Belmont, California. 536 pp.

Milner, C.A. 1989. *Major problems in the history of the American West.* Heath and Company, Lexington, Massachusetts. 681 pp.

Milstein, M. 1995. *Wolf return to Yellowstone.* The Billings Gazette, Billings. 96 pp.

Moulton, C. V. 1994. *Legacy of the Tetons: Homesteading in Jackson Hole.* Tamarack Books, Boise. 236 pp.

Murie, A. 1940. *Ecology of the coyote in Yellowstone.* Fauna of National Parks. 4:1-206.

Murie, O. J. 1951. *The elk of North America.* Stackpole, Harrisburg. 376 p.

Murie, O. J. 1935. *Food habits of the coyote in Jackson Hole, Wyoming.* U.S.D.A. Circular 362. 98 pp.

Nash, R. 1967. *Wilderness and the American mind.* Yale University Press, New Haven. 256 pp.

National Park Service. 1983. *Grand Teton: Official National Park Handbook.* National Park Service, Washington. 95 pp.

Nelson, F. K. 1994. *This was Jackson's Hole: Incidents and profiles from the settlement of Jackson Hole.* High Plains Press, Glendo, Wyoming. 380 pp.

Nowlin, D. D. 1904. *Annual report of the Wyoming Game and Fish Commission.* Cheyenne. 26 pp.

Nowlin, D. D. 1909. *Annual report of the Wyoming Game and Fish Commission.* Cheyenne. 39 pp.

Odum, E. P. 1969. *The strategy of ecosystem development.* Science 164:262-270.

Odum, E. P. 1971. *Fundamentals of ecology.* Saunders, Philadelphia. 574 pp.

Olson, L. L., and T. Bywater. 1991. *A Guide to exploring Grand Teton National Park.* RNM Press, Salt Lake City. 146 pp.

Ortenburger, L. 1965. *A climbers guide to the Teton Range.* Sierra Club, San Francisco. 336 pp.

Overton, W. S. 1971. *Estimating the numbers of animals in wildlife populations.* Pp. 403-455 in R. H. Giles, ed., Wildlife management techniques. The Wildlife Society, Washington.

Palmer, T. 1991. *The Snake River: Window to the West.* Island Press, Washington. 322 pp.

Parker, M. 1975. *Nutrient limitations of aquatic primary production in Grand Teton National Park.* Unpublished Mansucript. 99 pp.

Passmore, J. 1974. *Man's responsibility for nature: Ecological problems and western traditions.* Charles Scribner's Son's, New York. 213 pp.

Patterson, A. J. 1996. *The effect of recreation on biotic integrity of small streams in Grand Teton National Park.* M. S. Thesis, University of Washington, Seattle. 99 pp.

Peters, R. L., and T. E. Lovejoy. 1992. *Global warming and biological diversity.* Yale University Press. New Haven. 386 pp.

Phillipson, J. 1966. *Ecological energetics.* St. Martin's Press, New York. 57 pp.

Pielou, E. C. 1977. *Mathematical ecology.* Wiley & Sons, New York. 385 pp.

Porter, C. L. 1962. *Vegetation zones in Wyoming.* University of Wyoming Agricultural Experimental Station Bulletin 402:8-13.

Power, T. M. 1991. *Ecosystem preservation and the ecology in the Greater Yellowstone area.* Conservation Biology 5:395-404.

Primm, S. A., P. Lichtman, and T. W. Clark. 1996. *Natural fire in a political environment: Lessons from Yellowstone's 1988 fires.* Northern Rockies Conservation Cooperative, Jackson, Wyoming. 38 pp.

Primm, S. A. 1996. *A pragmatic approach to grizzly bear conservation.* Conservation Biology 10:1,026-1,035.

Putman, R. J., and S. D. Wratten. 1984. *Principles of ecology.* University of California Press, Berkeley. 388 pp.

Preble, E. A. 1911. *Report on condition of elk in Jackson Hole, Wyoming, in 1911.* U.S.D.A. Biological Survey Bulletin 40:1-23.

Pyne, S. 1982. *Fire in America: A cultural history of wildland and rural fire.* Princeton University Press, Princeton. 398 pp.

Raynes, B. 1995. *Valley so sweet.* White Willow Publishing, Jackson, Wyoming. 177 pp.

Raynes, B. 1984. *Birds of Grand Teton National Park.* Grand Teton Natural History Association, Moose, Wyoming. 90 pp.

Raynes, B., and M. Raynes. 1984. *Birds of Jackson Hole: A checklist.* Grand Teton Natural History Association, Moose, Wyoming. 15 pp.

Raynes, B., and D. Wile. 1994. *Finding the birds of Jackson Hole: A bird finding guide.* Published by D. Wile, Jackson, Wyoming. 157 pp.

Reed, J. F. 1952. *The vegetation of the Jackson Hole Wildlife Park, Wyoming.* American Midland Naturalist 48:700-729.

Reese, R. 1991. *Greater Yellowstone: The national park and adjacent wildlands.* American & World Geographic Publishing, Helena, Montana. 103 pp.

Righter, R. W. 1990. *A Teton country anthology.* Roberts Rinehart, Boulder, Colorado. 196 pp.

Roffee, T., and B. L. Smith. 1992. *Will it infect wild elk? Tuberculosis.* Bugle (fall):87-92.

Rumely, J. H. 1966. *A synecological study of the forested moraines of the valley floor of Grand Teton National Park, Wyoming.* Ph.D. Thesis, Montana State University, Bozeman. 101 pp.

Salt, G. W. 1957. *An analysis of avifaunas in the Teton Mountains of Jackson Hole, Wyoming.* Condor 59:373-393.

Sanborn, M. 1978. *The Grand Tetons: The story of taming the western wilderness.* Homestead Press, Moose, Wyoming. 314 pp.

Saylor, D. J. 1971. *Jackson Hole, Wyoming: In the shadow of the Tetons.* University of Oklahoma Press, Norman. 268 pp.

Schaller, G. B. and G. R. Lowther. 1969. *The relevance of carnivore behavior to the study of early hominids.* Southwestern Journal of Anthropology 25:307-341.

Schmidt, K. J. 1990. *Conserving Greater Yellowstone: A teacher's guide.* Northern Rockies Conservation Cooperative, Jackson, Wyoming. 232 pp.

Schmidt, J., and T. Schmidt. 1996. *Grand Teton: Citadels of stone.* Harper Collins, New York. 132 pp.

Schumacher, E. F. 1973. *Small is beautiful: A study of economics as if people mattered.* Blond and Briggs, London. 287 pp.

Sears, P. B. 1959. *The steady-state: Physical laws and moral choices.* The Key Reporter 24:2.

Shaw, R. J. 1974. *Plants of Yellowstone and Grand Teton National Parks.* Wheelwright Press, Salt Lake City. 159 pp.

Shaw, R. J. 1976. *Field guide to the vascular plants of Grand Teton National Park and Teton County, Wyoming.* Utah State University Press, Logan. 301 pp.

Shaw, R. J. 1992a. *Wildflowers of Grand Teton and Yellowstone National Parks including the Greater Yellowstone Ecosystem.* Wheelwright Press, Salt Lake City. 64 pp.

Shaw, R. J. 1992b. *Vascular plants of Grand Teton National Park and Teton County: An annotated checklist.* Grand Teton Natural History Association, Moose, Wyoming. 92 pp.

Sholley, D. R., and S. M. Newman. 1991. *Guardians of Yellowstone: An intimate look at the challenges of protecting America's foremost wilderness park.* William Morrow and Co., New York. 317 pp.

Simpson, G. G. 1962. *Evolution's two components: Biological and cultural.* Science 136:142-143.

Slotkin, R. 1992. *Gunfighter nation: The myth of the frontier in twentieth-century America.* Harper Perennial, New York. 850 pp.

Sladen, B. K., and F. B. Bangs, eds. 1969. *Biology of populations.* American Elsevier, New York. 449 pp.

Smith, H. W. 1952. *Man and his gods.* Grosset and Dunlap, New York. 501 pp.

Smith, R. L. 1977. *Elements of ecology and field biology.* Harper and Row, New York. 497 pp.

Smith, B. L. 1996. *Migratory behavior of the Jackson elk herd.* Yellowstone Science 3(4):6-10.

Smith, B. L., and R. L. Robbins. 1994. *Migrations and management of the Jackson Hole elk herd.* U.S. Department of Interior, National Biological Survey, Resource Publication 199:1-61.

Smith, B. L., and T. Roffee. 1992. *A political disease—Brucellosis.* Bugle (Summer):71-80.

Soil Conservation Service. 1982. *Soil survey of Teton County, Wyoming, Grand Teton National Park area.* U.S. GPO, Washington. 173 pp. + maps.

Southwick, C. H. 1976. *Ecology and the quality of our environment.* Van Nostrand, New York. 426 pp.

Stelfox, J. B., and L. Lawrence. 1991. *A field guide to the hoofed mammals of Jackson Hole.* Teton Science School, Kelly, Wyoming. 50 pp.

Stoltenberg, C. H., K. D. Ware, R. J. Marty, R. D. Wray, and J. D.Wellons. 1970. *Planning research for resource decisions.* Iowa State University Press, Ames. 183 pp.

Streubel, D. P. 1989. *Small mammals of the Yellowstone Ecosystem.* Robert Rinehart, Boulder, Colorado. 152 pp.

Sweeney, J. M. 1990. *Management of dynamic ecosystems.* Proceedings of a Symposium, 51st Midwest Fish and Wildlife Conference, Springfield, Illinois 180 pp.

Taylor, D. T. 1976. *Birds and forest fires: The tree hole nesting cycle.* Teewinot (GTNP newspaper) 1:3.

Teton County. 1994. *Jackson/Teton County comprehensive plan.* Jackson, Wyoming. 1,367 pp.

Thomas, W. L., ed. 1956. *Man's role in changing the face of the earth.* University of Chicago Press, Chicago. 1,193 pp.

Toynbee, A. 1972. *The religious background of the present environmental crises.* International Journal of Environmental Studies 3:642-643.

Ultseh, G. R. 1973. *Man in balance with the environment: Pollution and the optimal population size.* BioScience 23:642-643.

University of Wyoming and National Park Service Research Center. 1994. *18th annual report.* Grand Teton National Park, Moose Wyoming. 165 pp.

U.S. Congress. 1985. *Oversight hearing on the Greater Yellowstone Ecosystem.* Committee on Interior and Insular Affairs, House of Representatives, GPO, Washington. 697 pp.

Verner, J. 1958. *Study of illumination intensities in four plant communities.* M. S. Thesis, University of Wyoming, Laramie. 35 pp.

Vogel, B. 1989. *Invertebrates.* Pp. 22-32 in T. W. Clark, A. H. Harvey, R. D. Dorn, D. L. Genter, and C. R. Groves, eds., Rare, sensitive, and threatened species of the Greater Yellowstone Ecosystem. Northern Rockies Conservation Cooperative, Montana Natural Heritage Program, The Nature Conservancy, and Mountain West Environmental Services. Jackson, Wyoming.

Watt, K. E. F. 1974. *The Titanic effect.* Sinauer Associates, Stamford, Connecticut. 268 pp.

Wheelis, A. 1971. *The end of the modern age.* Harper and Row, New York. 129 pp.

Whitaker, R. H. 1970. *Communities and ecosystems.* Macmillan, New York, 162 pp.

White, L., Jr. 1967. *The historical roots of our ecological crises.* Science 155:1,203-1,207.

Wienere, C. 1996. *Jackson Hole: Crossroads of the west.* American and World Geographic Publishing, Helena. 103 pp.

Wile, D. 1996. *Identifying and finding the mammals of Jackson Hole (including Grand Teton National Park): A field guide.* Published by D. Wile, Jackson, Wyoming. 139 pp.

Wilkinson, T. 1991. *Greater Yellowstone: National Forests.* Falcon Press, Helena, Montana. 104 pp.

Wilson, E. O., ed. 1988. *Biodiversity.* National Academy Press, Washington. 521 pp.

Wright, G. A. 1976. *The coming of the people.* Naturalist 27:8-19.

Wright, G. A., and S. A. Reeve. 1976. *A preliminary report on Two Ocean Lake 1 (48 TE 357): A seasonal camp in Grand Teton National Park.* Manuscript on file at Midwest Archaeological Center, Lincoln, Nebraska.

World Commission on Environment and Development. 1987. *Our common future.* Oxford University Press, New York. 400 pp.

Wynne-Edwards, V. C. 1962. *Animal dispersal in relation to social behavior.* Hafner, New York. 653 pp.

Wuerthner, G. 1988. *Yellowstone and the fires of change.* Haggis House, Salt Lake City. 234 pp.

Yaffee, S. L., A. F. Phillips, I. C. Frentz, P. W. Hardy, S. M. Maleki, and B. E. Thorpe. 1996. *Ecosystem management in the United States: An assessment of current experience.* Island Press,Washington. 269 pp.

Yandell, M. D. 1976. *National parkways Grand Teton National Park.* World-Wide Research and Publishing, Casper, Wyoming. 68 pp.

Yorgason, I. J., and G. F. Cole. 1967. *Elk migration study. Jackson Hole Elk Herd.* Wyoming Game and Fish Commission and National Park Service. Mimeo. 15 pp.

Index

Jackson Hole Conservation Alliance, 73-74

Jackson Hole Land Trust, 74

Jackson Lake, 11-12; dam, 11

Juniper community, 44

K-selected species, 23

Knight, Dennis, 37

Lakes, 11-12

Land use planning, 73

Life history, 23

Limits of tolerance, 22

Linnaeus, Carl, 14

Lodgepole pine community, 41-42

Lower plants, 15

Mammals, 20-21

Marten, see American marten

Meadow community, 38, 68

Moose, 29-30

Mountain formation, 6-7

Mule deer, 27-29

Murie, Olaus, 3

Mutualism, 46

National Elk Refuge, 25-27

Native Americans, 1, 63-64

Niche theory, 46

Northern Rockies Conservation Cooperative, 74

Omnivores, 52

Organization of matter, 2-3

Ozone shield, 68-69

Paleoecology, 50

Parasitism, 46

Photosynthesis, 53

Physical environment, 5-13

Physiography, 5-6

Plants, 15

Population ecology, 25-35; principles, 31-33

Population regulation, 32-33; elk, 27;

humans, 67; moose, 30

Precipitation, 9

Predation, 46-47

President's Council on Sustainable Development, 70

Producers, 52

Productivity, 53

Public policy, 73

Pyramids of energy and numbers, 54-55

Quality of life, 71-72

r-selected species, 23

Reptiles, 19-20

Restoration ecology, 59-61

Rio Conference, 70

Rivers, 11-12

Sagebrush community, 39-40

Scientific names, 14

Sense of place, 71

Shaw, Richard, 15

Small mammals, 21

Snake River, 1, 12; Canada geese, 31; fisheries, 18-19

Snow, 9-10, 71

Soils, 10-11

Species concept, 14

Species diversity, 45-46, 56-57

Spruce-fir community, 43-44

Succession, see ecological succession

Sustainable development, 70-75

Taxonomy, 14

Temperature, 9

Territories, 33

Teton County land use planning, 71, 73

Teton Mountain Range, 1, 5-8, 65

Teton Wilderness, 1, 12

Theory, 4

Thermus aquaticus, 57

Tourism, 1, 66

Toxic elements (table), 68

Tree-hole nesting cycle, 48-49

Turnover of lake water, 11-12

Vascular plants, 15

Vision exercise, 72

West Gros Ventre Butte, 5; wintering mule deer, 28-29

Wildflowers, 15

Willow community, 38

Wind, 10

Wolves, 21; elimination from ecosystem, 34; restoration, 60-61

World Commission on Environment and Development, 70

World Conservation Strategy, 70

Yellowstone National Park, 1; biological isolation, 58; establishment, 65; wolves reintroduced, 61

About the Author

Tim Clark is professor adjunct in the School of Forestry and Environmental Studies and fellow in the Institution for Social and Policy Studies, Yale University. He is also board president of the Northern Rockies Conservation Cooperative in Jackson, Wyoming. He received his Ph.D. from the University of Wisconsin-Madison in 1973. His interests include conservation biology, organization theory and management, and the policy sciences. He has written over 300 papers, including a recent one addressing interdisciplinary problem solving in the Greater Yellowstone Ecosystem. His several books and monographs include *Mammals in Wyoming* (co-author, 1987), *Conservation Biology of the Black-Footed Ferret* (1989), *Tales of the Grizzly* (co-author, 1993), *Greater Yellowstone's Future: Prospects for Ecosystem Science, Management, and Policy* (1994), *Averting Extinction: Reconstructing Endangered species Recovery* (1997), and *Carnivores in Ecosystems: The Yellowstone Experience* (co-edited, *1999*). He has received various awards, including the Outstanding Contribution Award from the U.S. Fish and Wildlife Service, the Presidential Award for the Chicago Zoological Society, and the Best Teacher from the students at the Yale School of Forestry and Environmental Studies. Tim has served as a member of the Policy Review Committee of Research and Resource Management in the U.S. National Park Service. He is also a member of three species survival commissions of the IUCN-World Conservation Union. For more than twenty-five years, he has dedicated himself to endangered species conservation in the U.S., Australia and elsewhere.